Children with Language Impairments

An Introduction

Morag L. Donaldson

Jessica Kingsley Publishers
London and Bristol, Pennsylvania

The right of Morag Donaldson to be identified as author of this work has been asserted by her in accordance with the Copyright, Designs and Patents Act 1988.

Based on a research report funded by the Scottish Office Education Department.

First published in the United Kingdom in 1995 by
Jessica Kingsley Publishers Ltd
116 Pentonville Road
London N1 9JB, England
and
1900 Frost Road, Suite 101
Bristol, PA 19007, U S A

Copyright © 1995 Jessica Kingsley Publishers

Library of Congress Cataloging in Publication Data
Donaldson, Morag L.
Children with language impairments : an introduction / Morag L. Donaldson.
p.   cm.
Includes bibliographical references and index.
ISBN 1-85302-313-2 (pb : alk. paper)
1. Language disorders in children. I. Title.
RJ496.L35D66   1995
618.92'855--dc20   95-16494
CIP

British Library Cataloguing in Publication Data
Donaldson, Morag L.
Children with Language Impairments:
Introduction
I. Title
618.92855

ISBN 1 85302 313 2

Printed and Bound in Great Britain by
Biddles Ltd, Guildford and King's Lynn

Contents

To my parents, Christina and Harry

Acknowledgements

This book originated in a report commissioned by the Scottish Office Education Department in 1991. Their support is gratefully acknowledged. Particular thanks are due to HMI Dr Michael Gibson for his advice and encouragement.

My interest in children with language impairments was initially aroused when Elizabeth Dean and Janet Howell asked me to collaborate with them in a research project, investigating the efficacy of the Metaphon approach to treating children with a phonological disorder (funded by the Medical Research Council). I thank Liz and Janet for this and for all that I have learned through our collaboration. Over the past few years, I have also enjoyed fruitful collaborations with my other colleagues on the Metaphon project and on subsequent research projects in the area of children's language impairments. For this I thank Robert Grieve, Sally Millar, Claire Murray, Jennifer Reid, Louise Tait and George Thomson.

Jennifer Reid deserves a special mention for contributing in many ways to this book. She provided insightful, constructive comments on earlier drafts and made many helpful suggestions for revisions. I have benefited greatly from her willingness to share her expertise as an experienced speech and language therapist. I thank Jen for her collaboration, practical help, friendship and encouragement.

CHAPTER 1

Introduction

1.1 Reflecting on Language Difficulties

For most of us, the task of learning to speak our first language was accomplished in early childhood with remarkable speed and ease, and without explicit tuition. There are some children, though, who experience difficulties in acquiring language, and it is with these children that this book is concerned.

When we attempt to acquire a second language at school or as adults, most of us become all too aware of how complex language is and of how demanding the task of language learning is. Although there are important differences between learning a first language as a child and learning a second language later in life, our ability to appreciate the problems faced by children with language impairments can sometimes be enhanced by reflecting on our experiences of second language learning. For example, if you are struggling to use and understand an unfamiliar language in a situation where all the other people present are fluent speakers of that language, then you may feel socially isolated and powerless. You may also feel that the other people in the group are under-estimating your intelligence because of the fact that you cannot express your thoughts adequately in their language. Since language serves important social and cognitive functions, the consequences of language impairment for a child are potentially far-reaching, both in educational settings and in other everyday situations.

Conversely, the factors which contribute to difficulties in using and understanding language appropriately are not always purely linguistic. Linguistic skills are complex and multi-faceted, requiring the coordination of a variety of skills from the perceptual, motor, cognitive and social domains. For example, in order to hold a successful conversation, we require not only semantic and syntactic abilities (such as choosing appropriate words and arranging them in the correct order), but also perceptual abilities (to perceive the differences between speech sounds), motor abilities (to articulate speech sounds), cognitive abilities (to remember what has already been said) and social abilities (to make our contribution relevant to the needs of the listener). Therefore there are many possible sources of problems in language acquisition.

This book aims to:

- provide an introductory overview of the nature of language impairments in children

- consider the interplay between linguistic problems and other aspects of development

- explore the implications for assessment and intervention, with particular emphasis on the heterogeneous nature of language impairments.

Before addressing these aims, I shall establish the terminological conventions to be used throughout the book and consider some issues of definition.

1. 2 Language and Communication

The terms 'language' and 'communication' are sometimes used as if they were synonymous. In one sense, the total set of children who have language disorders coincides fairly closely with the total set of children who have communication disorders. Since language is one of the main tools with which communication is accomplished, children who have language problems will often have communication problems too. And since communication is one of the main functions of language, children who have communication problems are likely to have difficulties in using language appropriately. Thus, the distinction between language and communication disorders is not crucial to a consideration of overall prevalence rates.

However, the distinction is important in gaining an understanding of the nature of the problems faced by different sub-groupings of children. Although language is an important means of communication, there are also non-linguistic means of communication, such as touch, gesture, facial expression, eye contact and gaze. Some children (most notably autistic children) have communication problems which affect both linguistic and non-linguistic means of communication, but a greater number of children have problems which are specific to linguistic communication. Yet another group of children have communication problems because of severe physical problems (such as cerebral palsy) which prevent them from producing spoken language. This type of communication problem can often be reduced by the introduction of appropriate alternative or augmentative communication systems (see section 6.2), although such systems tend to be less widely understood, less socially acceptable and/or less flexible and convenient than spoken language.

Conversely, communication is not the only function which language fulfils. Language can also be a powerful cognitive tool, serving as a means of mental representation and hence influencing children's thinking and memory. Therefore, the difficulties encountered by children who have language impairments will not necessarily be confined to the area of communication.

In this book, the main focus will be on language impairments, but we will also consider their impact on communication and the extent to which they are accompanied by problems of non-linguistic communication for particular groups of children.

1.3 Language, Spoken Language and Speech

Some authors restrict the term 'language impairments' to problems other than those of pronunciation, which are referred to as 'speech disorders' or 'articulation disorders'. Other authors use 'language impairments' in a more inclusive way to cover all types of problem, whether these relate to speech sounds, grammar or vocabulary. Yet others use 'speech disorders' in this more general way to refer to any type of problem with spoken language. Here, the term 'language impairments' will be used to include rather than to contrast with 'speech disorder' (which will be restricted to difficulties in producing speech sounds).

Although the emphasis in the literature on language impairments is on spoken language, it is important to remember that language can also take the form of written language or sign language (such as British Sign Language). In this book, it should be assumed that 'language' refers to spoken language, unless otherwise specified.

1.4 Impairment, Disorder, Delay and Deviance

These terms are sometimes used more or less interchangeably. However, some authors make a distinction between 'language delay' (where language development is simply slower than average and errors are typical of those which would be made by a younger child) and 'language impairment'/'language disorder' (where language development is qualitatively different from the norm and errors are deviant compared to those produced by children of any age). This distinction is theoretically interesting, but very difficult to implement in practice. Therefore, I shall adopt the more general interpretation of 'impairment' and 'disorder' which is neutral with respect to the delayed/deviant distinction. Where a contrast is required, I shall distinguish between 'delayed' and 'deviant' patterns of linguistic development. The terms 'impairment' and 'disorder' will be used interchangeably.

1.5 Standards of Comparison

As with all aspects of development, children vary in terms of the speed at which their language develops. This raises the question of how the dividing line should be drawn between 'normal' and 'impaired' language development. There is no easy answer to this question, and different researchers have adopted different approaches to arriving at an answer. These approaches can be broadly categorized as either criterion-referenced or norm-referenced.

In a criterion-referenced approach, a child's language performance is compared to a criterion or goal, such as 'successful communication' or 'intelligibility'. For example, in the National Child Development Study, speech disorders were identified on the basis of teachers' and doctors' ratings of the intelligibility of children's speech (Sheridan, 1973).

A norm-referenced approach involves comparing a child's language performance with that of other children, rather than with an extrinsic standard. Many researchers have defined language impairment by comparing children's performance on a standardized language test to that of other children of the same age. The dividing line between normal and impaired language has been drawn at a variety of points, such as two standard deviations below the mean (Silva, 1980), one standard deviation below the mean (Beitchman, Nair, Clegg and Patel, 1986), or at the fifth percentile (Silva, McGee and Williams, 1983). In other words, these varying dividing lines define language impaired children in terms of the lowest-scoring 2.3 per cent, 16 per cent or 5 per cent of an age group, respectively. (It should be noted that an element of circularity is introduced when this approach is used in determining prevalence rates of language impairments – see Chapter 3.)

An alternative technique for interpreting norm-referenced test scores is to convert a child's score to an age-equivalent score, which corresponds to the average age of the children who obtained that same score. Language impairment can then be defined in terms of the extent to which the child's language age lags behind her or his chronological age. However, there is no theoretically sound way of deciding on the length of lag which constitutes a language impairment. Indeed, Lahey (1988; 1990) cautions against the use of age-equivalent scores in identifying language impairment, since they fail to take account of the range of variability within an age group and also since the amount of delay which should be considered problematical is likely to vary from age to age.

Yet another version of the norm-referenced approach involves comparing a child's language score to the language scores obtained by other children of the same mental age (rather than the same chronological age). The rationale behind this approach is that children should be classed as language impaired only if their language abilities are poor in comparison with their level of intelligence. For example, according to this approach, a five-year-old child who had a language age of three years would not be considered to have a language impairment if an intelligence test revealed that her mental age was also only three years. Lahey (1990) argues strongly against this approach on several grounds. First, as already noted, there are methodological problems with the use of age-equivalent scores. Second, it has been argued that intelligence is a multi-dimensional rather than a unidimensional construct (Gardner, 1983), and so it is difficult to decide which type of intelligence provides the most relevant comparison point. Third, theoretical claims about relationships between cognitive and linguistic development are not usually based on evidence from the types of tasks used in intelligence tests. Finally, there is, in any case, controversy about the extent to which cognitive development constrains linguistic development. (See section 6.5 for further discussion of this point, with particular reference to issues of intervention.) In view of these arguments, it would seem to be premature to restrict our definition of 'language impairment' to cases where the language problems are inconsistent with the child's level of intelligence. Instead, I shall follow the relatively common practice of referring to such cases as instances of 'specific language impairment' (see section 2.5), while retaining the more general definition of 'language impairment'.

CHAPTER 2

Categorizing Language Impairments

Language impairments are very diverse, and it is generally recognized that there is as yet no entirely satisfactory classification system. While it probably is not useful to attempt to assign a child's language problems to a rigid category, it is important to consider how one child's language problems compare with those of other children so that intervention can be informed by a professional's previous experience, by sharing of experiences amongst professionals and by the research literature.

There are two main types of approach to categorizing language impairments: the medical approach and the linguistic approach. The medical approach bases categorization primarily on the supposed aetiology of an impairment, whereas the linguistic approach bases categorization on the particular aspects of language behaviour which are affected by an impairment. Bishop and Rosenbloom (1987) argue that these two approaches should be regarded as complementary and that they can usefully be combined to yield a two-dimensional classification system. We shall briefly consider each of the dimensions in turn, before looking at how they inter-relate.

2.1 The Medical Approach

On the medical factors dimension of their taxonomy, Bishop and Rosenbloom distinguish seven aetiologically based categories in which children's language disorders are classed as being primarily due to:

(1) structural or sensorimotor defects of the speech apparatus (e.g. cleft palate; cerebral palsy)

(2) hearing loss

(3) brain damage or dysfunction acquired prenatally or perinatally (e.g. due to chromosomal disorders such as Down's syndrome)

(4) brain damage or dysfunction acquired in childhood (e.g. localized brain lesions resulting from head injuries)

(5) emotional/behavioural disorders (e.g. elective mutism)

(6) environmental deprivation (e.g. as suffered by children who are brought up in an institution where social interaction is severely limited)

(7) unclear aetiological factors (giving rise to disorders which are typically referred to as 'specific language impairments', 'specific language disorders', 'specific developmental language disorders' or 'developmental dysphasias').

An understanding of the likely origins of a child's language impairment can help to guide intervention. For many types of language impairment, effective intervention requires collaboration amongst different professionals (such as speech and language therapists, teachers, psychologists, audiologists, paediatricians, neurologists and physiotherapists); and the nature of this collaboration will often depend partly on the aetiology of the child's difficulties. A related point is that the aetiology of a child's language impairment will often have implications in terms of whether there are likely to be associated problems in other areas of development and in terms of the nature of such problems.

However, it is important to recognize the limitations of the medical approach. First, there is not a one-to-one correspondence between aetiological category and the nature of the child's linguistic difficulties. Within a given aetiological category, considerable variation typically exists in the characteristics and extent of children's problems with language. Conversely, similar linguistic difficulties can arise for children who have been assigned to different aetiological categories. Second, there is the issue of how far back in the causal chain one should search for the aetiology of a child's linguistic problems. For example, some children's linguistic difficulties are attributable to autism, which is thought to be caused by brain damage or dysfunction acquired prenatally or perinatally (Aitken, Papoudi, Robarts and Trevarthen, 1993). However, autism could also be classed as an emotional/behavioural disorder. Similarly, hearing loss and structural/sensorimotor defects of the speech apparatus can themselves be traced back to underlying causes of varying types. Thus, as Bishop and Rosenbloom point out, the categories are not necessarily mutually exclusive and they involve a combination of aetiological and functional criteria. Third, as the final category listed above indicates, it is not always possible to determine the aetiology of a child's linguistic difficulties. For these reasons, aetiological factors are best regarded as providing a useful framework within which to think about possible sources of language impairments, rather than as a rigid set of watertight categories. In particular, it is important to combine consideration of possible causes with consideration of the linguistic characteristics of the child's difficulties, and it is to this that we now turn.

2.2 The Linguistic Approach

Detailed analysis of the linguistic problems encountered by an individual child is a crucial step in identifying goals of intervention (see section 6.2). A useful backdrop for such analysis is provided by the linguistic approach to classification of language impairments. The linguistic dimension of classification can be further sub-divided into three dimensions. First, a distinction is drawn between **expressive** (or production) impairments and **receptive** (or comprehension) impairments. Expressive impairments affect the child's own use of language; that is, they apply to the child in the role of speaker. Receptive impairments affect the child's understanding of what other people are saying; that is, they apply to the child in the role of hearer. Sometimes both the receptive and the expressive functions of language will be affected. This will be referred to as a 'general language impairment/disorder'.

Cutting across the expressive/receptive distinction is a second set of distinctions relating to the level of the language system which is impaired. Four types of problem are usually distinguished:

(1) **Phonological** problems occur when the child has difficulty producing and/or perceiving contrasts between speech sounds. For example, a child with a phonological problem may fail to distinguish between the spoken words *key* and *tea*.

(2) **Syntactic** problems affect the child's ability to produce grammatical sentences and/or to respond appropriately to the grammatical properties of other people's speech. For example, a child with a receptive syntactic problem may treat a passive sentence like *The boy was chased by the girl* as if it was an active sentence, namely *The boy chased the girl.*

(3) **Semantic** problems consist of difficulties in expressing and/or understanding meaning through language. For example, the child may have a limited vocabulary or may have an incorrect understanding of the meaning of particular words.

(4) **Pragmatic** problems are impairments in the child's ability to use language to fulfil various communicative purposes and/or in the ability to recognize the communicative intent underlying other people's uses of language. For example, an autistic child may imitate another speaker's question instead of answering it.

Bishop and Rosenbloom propose a third dimension which distinguishes between **immature** (or delayed) and **deviant** patterns of disorder (see section 1.4). Combining all three dimensions of linguistic classification yields a total of sixteen types of disorder. However, these can be collapsed to give six broad groupings of language disorder, namely:

(1) speech limited in quality and/or quantity but other language skills normal;

(2) generalized delay of language development;

(3) specific problems with syntax and phonology;

(4) specific problems with semantics and pragmatics;

(5) poor understanding and limited verbal expression;

(6) severe impairment of non-verbal as well as verbal
      communication.

2.3 Combining the Medical and Linguistic Taxonomies

In planning intervention for individual children with language
impairments, it is important to combine the medical and linguistic
approaches by asking two types of question:

- What might be the cause of the child's language
  impairment?

- What are the linguistic characteristics of the child's
  problems?

To illustrate the interplay between the medical and linguistic
taxonomies, these same two questions can be asked about groups
of children with similar types of problems. On the aetiological
dimension, a broad distinction can be drawn between children
whose language problems appear to be secondary to other types of
problems (corresponding to the first six categories of Bishop and
Rosenbloom's medical taxonomy) and children whose problems
appear to be more specifically linguistic (corresponding to Bishop
and Rosenbloom's seventh category). In the remainder of this
chapter, we shall look at some of the sub-categories which tend to
be used in clinical and educational settings to group children under
these two broad headings. The aim will be to give a flavour of the
diversity and complexity of language impairments, in terms of both
aetiology and linguistic characteristics, rather than to provide a fully
comprehensive catalogue of language impairments.

2.4 Children with Secondary Language Impairments

To say that a linguistic problem is secondary to another problem does not imply that the linguistic problem is necessarily less severe either than the other problem or than a specific linguistic problem. Rather, it means that the linguistic problem is believed to be explicable (at least partially) in terms of the non-linguistic problem. The groupings under this heading are based mainly on aetiological/functional criteria but, as we shall see, some of the groupings are narrower than Bishop and Rosenbloom's medical categories.

Children with Cerebral Palsy

Cerebral palsy is a neurological disorder which gives rise to motor impairments, varying in degree of severity and in the parts of the body which are affected. Some children with cerebral palsy are able to speak normally, but others have impaired control of the muscles involved in speech production resulting in articulation problems (dysarthria) or in a complete inability to speak (anarthria). Thus, in terms of Bishop and Rosenbloom's medical taxonomy, cerebral palsy could be classed either as involving a sensorimotor defect of the speech apparatus or as arising from brain damage/dysfunction acquired prenatally or perinatally. The precise characteristics of the articulation problems vary. However, Cantwell and Baker (1987) report that consonants are more likely to be affected than vowels, that children with dysarthria typically speak slowly, and that intelligibility decreases markedly if they try to speak more quickly. In many cases, there are associated problems with feeding behaviours, such as sucking and chewing. There is also variation in whether or not the expressive language problems are accompanied by receptive language problems, and the situation is complicated by the fact that children with cerebral palsy sometimes also have intellectual impairments or hearing problems. On the basis of a review of the research evidence, Bishop (1993) concludes that children whose expressive language problems are related to cerebral palsy (or other physical problems) typically have receptive language abilities which are within the normal range, so long as their hearing and intelligence are also normal. Since the difficulties encountered by children with cerebral palsy relate mainly to the physical aspects of speech production, it is important to consider introducing alternative or augmentative systems of communication (see section 6.2).

Children with a Hearing Loss

The impact of a hearing loss on children's language skills varies according to a range of factors, including the child's age at onset and at diagnosis, the severity of the hearing loss, whether the child's parents are deaf or hearing and the nature of the child's linguistic environment (e.g. relative degrees of exposure to spoken language and sign language).

If children become deaf after they have acquired language, then (apart from the self-evident difficulties in perceiving speech) the effects are usually limited to relatively superficial speech problems, such as atypical intonation and voice quality and minor articulation difficulties. In contrast, children who are born deaf or who become deaf before they have acquired language (referred to as 'prelingually deaf children') typically have much more serious problems in acquiring spoken language. These children have to rely on a combination of residual hearing (often with artificial amplification) and visual input from lip-reading. Not surprisingly, the process of learning a spoken language tends to be slower and more laborious for prelingually deaf children than for children with normal hearing, and so delayed (and sometimes deviant) patterns of development have been reported for all aspects of language – phonological, syntactic, semantic and pragmatic (Mogford, 1993). Furthermore, the effects of hearing loss on language development sometimes extend to written language or to signed analogues of spoken English (Bishop and Rosenbloom, 1987).

On the other hand, in cases where deaf children are born to deaf parents and learn sign language as their first language, the rate of sign language development is similar to that for hearing children acquiring spoken language and may even be faster in some respects (Bonvillian, Orlansky and Novack, 1983; Bellugi, van Hoek, Lillo-Martin and O'Grady, 1993). (There is considerable debate about the most appropriate communication systems to use with deaf children, especially since the majority of deaf children have hearing parents and not all deaf parents are fluent in sign language – see section 6.2.)

The relationship between severity of hearing loss and severity of language impairment does not appear to be straightforward. Although the most severe levels of hearing loss generally result in the highest degrees of oral language impairment, for moderate or mild hearing impairments the correlation with severity of linguistic disorder is much less strong (Davis, Elfenbein, Schum and Bentler, 1986).

It has sometimes been suggested that there may be an increased risk of language impairments not only in children who have a permanent hearing loss but also in children who suffer from intermittent episodes of conductive hearing loss associated with middle ear disorders, such as otitis media. However, the evidence available at present implies that otitis media does not represent a strong risk factor (Klein and Rapin, 1993).

Children with Moderate or Severe Learning Difficulties

Children in this group (who are sometimes referred to as 'children with a mental handicap' or as 'children with a general developmental delay') have an IQ (intelligence quotient) which is below the normal range. They are usually characterized as having general difficulties across all intellectual domains or as having global delays in their cognitive development. Bishop and Rosenbloom (1987) discuss this group of children under the heading of 'brain damage or dysfunction acquired prenatally or perinatally', although they acknowledge that the underlying causes are varied and not always specifiable. General learning difficulties are often associated with language impairments, although, as Rutter and Lord (1987) point out, the presence of general learning difficulties does not in itself explain a child's language problems. While some children with learning difficulties show language impairments which are consistent with the extent of their general intellectual impairment, others have more severe problems with language than with other aspects of cognitive functioning. In particular, children with Down's syndrome (a chromosomal disorder) sometimes have linguistic problems which are disproportionate to their general cognitive difficulties (Dodd, 1976; Messer, 1994), perhaps partly because they have an increased incidence of hearing problems (Bishop and Rosenbloom, 1987).

Conversely, some children with learning difficulties show linguistic skills which are far superior to what would be expected on the basis of their general cognitive skills. For example, children with Williams syndrome (a rare metabolic disorder resulting in cognitive impairments) have been found to have linguistic abilities which, although delayed relative to their chronological ages, are clearly in advance of their non-linguistic abilities (Bellugi, Marks, Bihrle and Sabo 1993). Similarly, there are several reports of hydrocephalic children with very low IQs who nevertheless demonstrate the ability to produce language which is correct and highly complex syntactically and which employs an impressive vocabulary (Tew, 1979; Cromer, 1991). However, these children (displaying what is known as the 'cocktail party syndrome'), typically perform very poorly on formal tests of language comprehension and the content of their spontaneous speech is often semantically or pragmatically odd in relation to the conversational context. As such cases illustrate, language disorders associated with learning difficulties do not always affect all aspects of linguistic functioning equally.

Although it may be tempting to think of the linguistic development of children with learning difficulties as being simply delayed, there is increasing recognition that this is likely to be an over-simplification. In particular, the evidence on language development in children with Down's syndrome suggests that there is a mixture of delay and deviance, and indeed that a straightforward dichotomy between delay and deviance is itself too simplistic (Rondal, 1987, 1993; Messer, 1994). Furthermore, the term 'language delay' implies that the problems are transient and that the individual will eventually catch up with his or her peers. For most children with Down's syndrome this is far from being the case, in that their language abilities do not usually develop beyond the level characteristic of non-delayed three-year-olds (Fowler, 1990), although there is considerable variation amongst individual children with Down's syndrome in the rate, pattern and eventual level of their linguistic development.

Children with Autism

Autism is another disorder which comes under the heading of 'brain damage or dysfunction acquired prenatally or perinatally' in Bishop and Rosenbloom's medical taxonomy. There is now a considerable body of evidence linking autism with abnormal brain development beginning prenatally (for a review see Aitken *et al.* 1993). At a different level of explanation, though, autism could also be regarded as an emotional/behavioural disorder. Hobson (1991), for example, argues that an inability to perceive other people's emotions is fundamental to the deficits associated with autism. Others argue that the primary deficit is a cognitive one, namely the lack of a theory of mind and hence of the ability to reason about other people's mental states, such as beliefs and intentions (Baron-Cohen, 1991).

Delayed or deviant communicative development is one of the defining characteristics of autism, the others being impaired social development, ritualistic or repetitive behaviours and onset before 30 months of age (Rutter, 1985). Rutter and Lord (1987) report that about 70 per cent to 80 per cent of autistic children also have significant learning difficulties and that about 50 per cent of autistic people (most of whom have severe learning difficulties) never develop functional speech.

There is a very wide range of linguistic skills within the group of children diagnosed as autistic. At one extreme are those who are completely mute, while at the other extreme are those few autistic children who manage to score within the average range on verbal tests by early adolescence. However, even the latter group typically continue to have problems in using language appropriately in conversations to fulfil communicative and social purposes. Indeed it is such deficits in the pragmatic and semantic aspects of language which are most characteristic of autistic children as a group, although many autistic children also have problems with other aspects of language. Thus, Rapin and Allen (1987) found that a group of autistic children showed a range of linguistic problems similar to that shown by a group of children with specific language impairments, but that the relative frequencies of the different types of problems differed somewhat between the two groups, with semantic-pragmatic problems being more frequent for the autistic group.

It is interesting to note that words referring to psychological states and mental processes (such as *think* and *know*) tend to be missing from autistic children's vocabularies (Tager-Flusberg, 1992; Jordan, 1993). This semantic deficit probably reflects (or perhaps even contributes to) the difficulty which these children have in thinking about other people's minds.

A common characteristic of autistic children's language is echolalia, which involves repeating what other people have said. This tendency to imitate (either immediately or after a delay) often results in autistic children building up a repertoire of phrases or sentences which they can reproduce in a superficially accurate way, but which they tend to produce in inappropriate contexts due to inadequate comprehension. There is some debate in the literature as to how echolalia should be interpreted. For example, to what extent do autistic children use echolalia with communicative intent? And is echolalia indicative of autistic children having a holistic rather than an analytical approach to language processing and production (Fay, 1993)?

As one would expect from the characteristics of the disorder, autistic children's communication problems are not confined to language but extend to non-linguistic aspects of communication, for example leading to difficulties in producing and interpreting gestures, facial expressions and intonation appropriately.

2.5 Children with Specific Language Impairments

This category of children is defined by exclusion. These children have language problems despite the fact that their development appears to be essentially normal in other respects. In other words, their language impairment cannot be attributed to other problems such as those associated with cerebral palsy, hearing loss, general learning difficulties or autism. Consequently, such children are said to have a specific language impairment (SLI) although, as we shall see, their difficulties are often not restricted to linguistic domains.

Searching for an Explanation of SLI

The question of how specific language impairments might be explained has generated a considerable amount of research and debate in recent years, but the underlying causes have remained elusive. (For reviews of such research see Leonard (1987), Miller (1991), Johnston (1991), Bishop (1992) and Reid and Donaldson

(1993).) Most of the studies in this area have involved comparing a group of children with SLI to a group of children with normal language development (NLD children) in terms of their perform-ance on various types of tasks. The rationale behind such studies is that if the SLI group is found to perform less well than the NLD group on a particular type of task, then a deficit in the ability measured by that task is a possible cause of specific language impairment.

There is variation across studies in the type of criterion used for selecting children for the NLD comparison (or control) group. Two of the most commonly used types of comparison group are:

(1) a chronological age-matched group, in which the NLD children are the same age as the SLI children (but are by definition at a higher level of language development);

(2) a language-matched group, in which the NLD children are at a similar level of language development to the SLI children (but are younger chronologically).

Each of these approaches has its limitations. With a chronological age-match, it is difficult to determine whether an observed differ-ence between the groups is a cause or a consequence of their differing levels of language ability. Comparisons between language-matched groups usually permit stronger claims to be made about underlying causes of SLI, but it is still worth recognizing that differences in performance may sometimes be attributable to such factors as the SLI children using different strategies because their experience differs (in both quantity and quality) or because their abilities are developing unevenly. Furthermore, since children with SLI often show uneven patterns of development across different areas of linguistic functioning (e.g. receptive versus expressive, syntactic versus semantic), selection of an appropriate language measure on which to match the two groups can be problematic. It is important to bear these complications in mind when considering research evidence regarding the underlying nature of SLI.

The explanations which have been proposed for SLI are many and various. While some explanations attribute SLI to factors which are truly specific to language, other explanations appeal to more general perceptual or cognitive factors. At first sight, the latter type of explanation may seem paradoxical, since SLI children are by definition children who are developing normally apart from their language problems. However, it is possible for SLI children's development to be within the 'normal' range on global measures such as IQ tests and yet for their performance to be measurably below that of NLD children when specific cognitive or perceptual skills are probed (usually with specially designed experimental tasks).

Tallal and her colleagues (Tallal, Stark and Curtiss, 1976; Tallal, Stark and Mellits, 1985) have presented convincing evidence that SLI children perform less well than NLD children on tasks involving the perception or sequencing of acoustic events when these are presented either in rapid succession or for brief durations. This finding applies not only to speech sounds but also to non-linguistic stimuli such as tones. Therefore, Tallal argues that the underlying deficit in SLI is an auditory perceptual one. Although Tallal's findings have been highly influential, there is some controversy in the literature regarding how well the postulated deficit can account for the patterns of linguistic difficulties typically observed in SLI children (Leonard, 1987; Curtiss and Tallal, 1991; Bishop, 1992). Furthermore, most of Tallal's work has involved age-matched rather than language-matched comparison groups (although she has studied NLD children from a variety of age groups and has found that not even the younger age groups perform in a similar way to the SLI group). A related difficulty is that NLD children younger than about four years six months (who presumably have language ages comparable to some of Tallal's SLI children) are unable to perform

Tallal's tasks, which raises questions about whether the tasks may be demanding skills other than those which they are designed to measure.

Bishop (1992) argues that the deficit underlying SLI may not be specific to auditory perception, but rather may reflect a more general cognitive limitation in information-processing capacity, such that SLI children will experience more difficulty than NLD children in situations where they have to integrate large amounts of information within limited time constraints. The effects of this type of processing limitation would be particularly evident for auditory tasks, because of the transient nature of auditory stimuli. However, as Bishop herself points out, such an explanation of SLI is probably too general and powerful, in that it has difficulty in accounting for the fact that SLI children do not have across-the-board cognitive impairments. More specific versions of the limited processing capacity hypothesis are therefore required.

An example of such a hypothesis is that vocabulary deficits in SLI children are attributable to poor phonological memory (Gathercole and Baddeley, 1990, 1993). Support for this hypothesis comes from Gathercole and Baddeley's research. They found that SLI children with vocabulary deficits performed less well than language-matched NLD children on tasks requiring the children to repeat nonsense words spoken by the researcher. Gathercole and Baddeley argue that the SLI children had problems in holding phonological material in their memories even for a very short time period and that these problems are likely to interfere with the ability to learn new words.

Another specific example of the limited processing capacity approach is Bishop's recent proposal that the disproportionate difficulty which many SLI children have with certain grammatical morphemes – such as the past tense (-*ed*) and third person singular (-*s*) inflections on verbs – might be due to their processing grammatical information slowly within a limited capacity system (Bishop, 1994).

The issue of why SLI children have particular difficulties with certain grammatical morphemes is currently a subject of lively debate. In contrast to the information processing account, some researchers have put forward explanations which are more specifically linguistic in that they attribute SLI children's morphological difficulties to innate deficits in abstract grammatical knowledge (Gopnik and Crago, 1991; Rice and Oetting, 1993). Such explanations are based on the theoretical assumption that children's cognitive apparatus includes a component (or 'module') which is innately specialized for the acquisition of language and which incorporates knowledge about the abstract grammatical properties of human languages (Chomsky, 1986).

An interesting angle on this issue is provided by cross-linguistic research. On the basis of evidence from English-speaking, Italian-speaking and Hebrew-speaking SLI children, Leonard and his colleagues argue that SLI children's acquisition of grammatical morphology is influenced by a combination of different types of factors (Leonard, Sabbadini, Leonard and Volterra, 1987; Leonard, McGregor and Allen, 1992; Leonard and Dromi, 1994).

Support for a perceptual or processing deficit account comes from the finding that SLI children have particular problems with morphemes which are unstressed or of brief duration, such as the past tense (-ed) and third person singular (-s) inflections on verbs in English. In addition, though, SLI children's problems seem to be reduced for morphemes which have clear semantic correlates. Thus, for example, in English the plural morpheme -s on nouns (e.g. cats) is less problematic than the phonetically identical third person singular morpheme -s on verbs (e.g. hits). It has been argued that this may be because the meaning which corresponds to the plural morpheme ('more than one') is typically more obvious (from contextual cues) and less complex than the meaning which corresponds to the third person singular morpheme ('an action carried out in the present by one person who is neither the speaker nor the hearer'). A further influence on SLI children's difficulties relates to the grammatical importance of morphological contrasts in a particular language system. Hebrew morphology is much more complex than English morphology. For example, in Hebrew all nouns, verbs and adjectives are inflected (on a number of dimensions such as number and gender) so bare stems without inflections do not occur, whereas in English bare stems without inflections occur quite frequently (e.g. *dog, give, red*). Yet Hebrew-speaking SLI children (unlike English-speaking SLI children) do not show poorer acquisition of morphology than children in a language-matched control group. This rather counter-intuitive finding suggests that SLI children are sensitive to the characteristics of the particular language they are learning (e.g. whether inflections or differences in word order play the more major role in conveying meaning) and that their limited processing resources are capable of being focused on the most functionally important aspects of the language system. Similarly, Lindner and Johnston (1992) found that English-speaking SLI children experienced more morphological problems than their German-speaking counterparts, which they attribute to the greater functional significance of morphology in German – German morphology conveys more information about the grammatical structure and meaning of sentences than English morphology does. Such findings sound a promising note since they simply imply that, even in the face of impairment, children's linguistic systems have a fair degree of resilience and flexibility.

Leonard's approach to morphological difficulties is interesting in that it emphasises the interplay between general perceptual/cognitive factors and more specifically linguistic factors. This reflects an increasing awareness in the research literature of the need to consider multiple and interacting causes of SLI, rather than to continue searching for a single underlying cause. A related point is that the importance of recognizing the heterogeneity of SLI and distinguishing between different sub-types is now generally acknowledged (Leonard *et al.* 1987; Bishop, 1992; Reid and Donaldson, 1993).

Sub-types of SLI

As yet, there is no generally accepted and validated typology of SLI, so there is some variation in the classification systems and terminology used by different researchers and practitioners. The most widely used approach is probably Rapin and Allen's typology, which was developed in the USA on the basis of detailed clinical observations of SLI and autistic children (Rapin and Allen, 1983, 1987). To illustrate the heterogeneity of SLI, Rapin and Allen's categories will be briefly described (excluding those categories which relate specifically to autism). Some of the main terminological variants are shown in parentheses.

Verbal auditory agnosia (or 'auditory imperception' or 'word deafness') is a severe (but relatively rare) receptive disorder in which the child is unable to understand language in the auditory channel but is usually able to understand visually presented language (such as writing and sign languages). As one would expect, this extreme deficit in receptive ability has serious consequences for expressive ability: children with this disorder typically are either mute or have extremely dysfluent speech with defective articulation. Because these children are unresponsive to speech, it may be erroneously suspected initially that they have a hearing loss.

Verbal dyspraxia (or 'articulatory dyspraxia' or 'dyspraxia') is primarily an expressive disorder characterized by dysfluent effortful speech, with short utterances and defective phonology. In extreme cases, children with verbal dyspraxia may even be mute. Despite their severe expressive problems, children with verbal dyspraxia usually have adequate or normal receptive abilities. As several researchers have noted, there is a considerable lack of clarity in the literature regarding the underlying nature of verbal dyspraxia, its developmental course and criteria for diagnosing it (including how to distinguish it from dysarthria) (Stackhouse, 1992; Stackhouse and Snowling, 1992; MorganBarry, 1994).

Phonologic programming deficit syndrome (or 'phonological disorder' in the UK) is also primarily an expressive disorder. Children with this disorder have much more fluent speech and longer utterances than those with verbal dyspraxia, but their speech has poor intelligibility due to defective phonology. One of the most widely used accounts of phonological disorders is the 'phonological processes' approach, which characterizes disordered speech in terms of simplifying processes that affect classes of sounds, rather than in terms of difficulties with individual speech sounds (Ingram, 1976; Grunwell, 1981). An example of a phonological process is the deletion of final consonants, such that *ball* is pronounced as if it were *ba* and *hat* as if it were *ha*. This process is relatively common in children with normal language development, but it usually disappears around the age of three years, whereas in children with a phonological disorder it may persist for longer. There are other phonological processes, such as deletion of word initial consonants, which do not typically occur in normal language development but which sometimes occur in children with language disorders. Dodd, Leahy and Hambly (1989) argue that children with phonological disorders vary in terms of whether their development is delayed (involving phonological processes typical of younger children) or deviant (involving phonological processes which are atypical of normal development). There is some evidence to suggest that deviant phonological processes are less likely to disappear sponta- neously (Leahy and Dodd, 1987).

Phonologic-syntactic deficit syndrome (or 'phonological-syntactic disorder' in the UK) involves similar problems to those associated with phonologic programming deficit syndrome, but the phonological problems are typically more severe (Bishop and Edmundson, 1987) and are accompanied by grammatical deficits. In particular, the speech of children with this syndrome tends to be lacking in function words (such as articles, pronouns and prepositions) and in morphological suffixes (such as the word endings that mark tense and number). Rapin and Allen regard this syndrome as entailing deficits in comprehension as well as production, although the comprehension problems tend to be less severe and more subtle than the expressive ones and therefore may sometimes be overlooked. Support for this argument comes from a study by Adams (1990) in which children who appeared to have purely expressive syntactic problems in spontaneous conversation were found to also have receptive problems, when their syntactic comprehension was assessed with a structured task. Since phonological problems are generally more readily resolved than grammatical ones, children who are initially diagnosed as having a phonological-syntactic disorder may show only grammatical problems at later stages of development.

Lexical-syntactic deficit syndrome (or 'lexical-syntactic disorder' in the UK) is typically diagnosed when a child has normal phonology, but is late to begin talking, has severe word finding problems, immature syntax and difficulties in producing connected, coherent language. The difficulties which these children have in retrieving appropriate words from their mental lexicons are often particularly evident in spontaneous conversation, and may take the form of long pauses (sometimes with fillers such as *er* or *em*), incorrect uses of words and circumlocutions (German and Simon, 1991).

Semantic-pragmatic deficit syndrome (or 'semantic-pragmatic disorder' in the UK) is characterized by children having more difficulty with the content and use of language than with its formal phonological and syntactic properties. The language problems which characterize these children are unusual in that they are often more evident in relatively unstructured conversational contexts than in formal tests, and in that comprehension sometimes appears to be inferior to production (Bishop and Rosenbloom, 1987; Bishop, 1989). For example, children with a semantic-pragmatic disorder tend to produce sentences which are correct in themselves but which are irrelevant or tangential in relation to preceding parts of the conversation, or which are based on over-literal interpretations of another person's speech (Adams and Bishop, 1989; Bishop and Adams, 1989). They may also have difficulties in taking turns appropriately in a conversation. They sometimes chatter incessantly and give echolalic responses. Some of these children have large vocabularies. On the other hand, they also have a tendency to use circumlocutions and they may fail to express meanings in a sufficiently specific way. These linguistic characteristics are similar to (although usually less severe than) those shown by autistic children. In other aspects of behaviour, too, children with semantic-pragmatic disorder sometimes show mild autistic features. It has been suggested that the characteristics of semantic-pragmatic disorder lie on a continuum which has autism at one extreme and normal communication at the other (Bishop and Rosenbloom, 1987; Bishop, 1989). The validity and usefulness of the category of semantic-pragmatic disorder have not gone unquestioned. For example, McTear and Conti-Ramsden (1992) argue that descriptions of semantic-pragmatic disorder tend to imply too clearcut a distinction between difficulties with language form and difficulties with language use, and thus fail to take account of the fact that some children do have pragmatic difficulties which are related to difficulties with language form. They further argue that important distinctions between semantic and pragmatic problems may be obscured by grouping both types of problem under a single label.

2.6 Overview and Implications

Language impairments are sometimes categorized according to their probable aetiological origins or according to the other types of problems to which they may be secondary (such as cerebral palsy, hearing loss, general learning difficulties and autism). Those language impairments which are not readily explained in such terms are typically assigned to the 'umbrella' category of specific language impairments, a category which is defined by exclusion of known causes. However, the distinction between secondary and specific language impairments is not entirely clearcut, so it may be more appropriate to think in terms of a continuum of specificity rather than a strict dichotomy. For instance, although attempts to identify underlying causes of specific language impairment have not yielded conclusive results as yet, it appears that a partial explanation at least may lie in cognitive/perceptual processing limitations. The medical/aetiological approach to classification needs to be combined with a linguistic approach in which children's language impairments are categorized according to the aspects of language ability which are affected (expressive/receptive; phonological/grammatical/semantic/pragmatic). A linguistically based classification system is important both in conducting research (for example into the underlying nature of SLI) and in designing appropriate interventions for individual children.

CHAPTER 3

Prevalence of Language Impairments in Children

3.1 Prevalence Studies

There have been several large-scale studies which have provided an indication of the percentage of children who have language impairments and of associations between language impairments and non-linguistic variables such as gender, social class, intelligence and behaviour problems. The results of the various studies are not always directly comparable because of differences in the way the studies were conducted. Studies have varied in such characteristics as the age of the children, the way the sample has been obtained (for example, by screening an entire population or by studying referrals to speech and language therapists), the assessment methods used, and the way 'language impairment' has been defined. Issues of definition are discussed more fully in Chapter 1. In general terms, though, studies have differed with respect to:

(1) whether they have taken 'language impairment' to include all or only some of the categories of articulation problems, other expressive language problems and receptive language problems;

(2) whether they have restricted 'language impairment' to cases where the impairment is specific to language rather than part of a more general problem such as learning difficulties;

(3) where they have drawn the dividing line between normal and impaired language, and between severe and more minor impairments.

A further problem is the shortage of prevalence data for specific categories of language impairment. Although there is general agreement amongst researchers that language disordered children do not represent a homogeneous group (see Chapter 2), prevalence estimates typically relate either to the group as a whole or to very broad sub-groupings.

3.2 Prevalence Rates

In the Dundee Development Screening Programme Research Project (Drillien and Drummond, 1983), approximately 5,000 children born in 1974 or 1975 and living in Dundee were assessed for neurodevelopmental disabilities, including language impairments. The findings indicated that 5.7 per cent of the children had a language impairment at some point between the ages of two and five years, and that for 4.2 per cent of the children the impairment was moderately severe or severe. However, these figures do not include children whose language problems had been classed as being part of another disability (such as hearing loss or motor disorder). Including these children increases the overall prevalence of language impairments to 7.5 per cent and the prevalence of moderately severe or severe language impairments to 4.4 per cent. When the group of children whose major disability was a language disorder were sub-categorized according to whether they showed an articulatory disorder, an expressive language delay or a comprehension delay, it was found that the percentage of children from the language impaired group falling into each of the categories was as follows:

articulatory disorder alone	36%
expressive language delay alone	29%
articulatory disorder and expressive language delay	21%
expressive language and comprehension delays	9%
all three types of problem	1%
nature of disorder unknown	5%

The prevalence rates found in the Dundee study are broadly consistent with those from studies carried out in other parts of the English-speaking world, although it is impossible to make straightforward comparisons for the reasons outlined in the previous section.

For example, Stevenson and Richman (1976) reported a prevalence rate of 3.1 per cent for expressive language disorder and of 2.3 per cent for severe expressive language disorder in their study of three-year-olds in Waltham Forest (an outer London borough). One obvious reason for these rates being lower than those in the Dundee study is that Stevenson and Richman focused on expressive language problems other than articulation problems, whereas Drillien and Drummond also included articulation and comprehension problems. Furthermore, the Waltham Forest figures relate specifically to problems identified at the age of three years, whereas the Dundee figures relate to problems identified at any point during the three year period between the ages of two and five years.

Silva, McGee and Williams (1983) found that 7.6 per cent of the three-year-olds they studied in Dunedin (New Zealand) had language impairments. Although this figure is virtually identical to that in the Dundee study, the relative frequencies of different types of impairment are inconsistent between the two studies. In the Dunedin study, 31 per cent of the language problems were in expressive language only, 34 per cent were in comprehension only and 34 per cent involved both expressive language and comprehension. Thus, in the Dunedin study, 68 per cent of the children with language impairments had problems with comprehension, in contrast to only 10 per cent in the Dundee study. This discrepancy may be partly because some children in the Dundee study with problems in both language comprehension and expression are likely to have been assigned to the category of 'global delay and mental retardation' rather than to the category of language disorder. Moreover, in the Dundee study, systematic assessment of expressive language and comprehension with a standardized test (see section 5.3) was carried out only for those children who were referred to a child development centre or a hospital for assessment. Since comprehension problems are typically less easily detected than production problems in everyday contexts, it is probable that children with problems primarily affecting comprehension would be less likely to be referred. In contrast, the Dunedin study involved administering a standardized test of language ability to a large sample of children irrespective of whether or not they had been referred with language problems. Therefore, the prevalence rates in the Dundee study for comprehension problems in particular and hence for language disorders in general may well be under-estimates.

On the basis of a review of prevalence studies, Silva (1987) concludes that estimates of the incidence of language impairments have ranged from 3 per cent to 15 per cent, with a median of about

6 to 8 per cent, and that most researchers agree on a prevalence rate of about 1 per cent for severe language impairments.

A limitation in the evidence on prevalence is that it relates almost entirely to the preschool period, although there are a few exceptions to this. In the National Child Development Study, it was found that between 10 per cent and 13 per cent of seven-year-olds had some degree of speech impairment, with between 1 per cent and 2 per cent having a severe impairment (Peckham, 1973). However, these data are restricted to doctors' and teachers' ratings of the intelligibility of children's speech. More comprehensive data are provided by Silva, McGee and Williams (1983) who report that in their Dunedin study 3.6 per cent of seven-year-olds showed a specific comprehension problem, 2.8 per cent showed a specific expression problem and 2 per cent showed a general language problem, giving a total of 8.4 per cent of seven-year-olds who showed some type of language impairment.

3.3 Gender

Several studies have found higher prevalence rates of language impairment in boys than in girls (Sheridan, 1973; Stevenson and Richman, 1976; Fundudis, Kolvin and Garside, 1979; Silva, 1980; Drillien and Drummond, 1983). In most of these studies, approximately twice as many boys as girls have been identified as having a language impairment.

3.4 Social Class

Although language impairments occur in all social classes, there is some evidence that they are over-represented in children from lower socio-economic status backgrounds (Peckham, 1973; Fundudis *et al.* 1979; Drillien and Drummond, 1983; Silva, Williams and McGee, 1987; Haynes and Naidoo, 1991). Drillien and Drummond

(1983) note that while their study showed only a slight trend towards a greater frequency of language impairments in lower social class groups, the true extent of this trend may have been masked by the fact that their sample was obtained through referrals, since middle class parents are more likely to seek professional advice.

3.5 Intelligence

In interpreting the findings reported in this section, it is important to bear in mind that they come from studies which investigated a random sample of children from the general population and which therefore included some children with general learning difficulties. In other words, the findings relate not only to children with specific language impairments but also to those whose language difficulties are associated with other more global problems.

Silva *et al.* (1983) found that 25 per cent of the seven-year-old children who had a language disorder also had a low general IQ, whereas only 13 per cent of the total sample of children had a low IQ. For children who had a language impairment affecting both expressive and receptive abilities, the prevalence of low IQ was even higher (40%). In a sense, the increased incidence of low IQ amongst children with language impairments is not surprising, since there are similarities between the items used in detecting language impairments and those used in the verbal scales of intelligence tests. However, Silva, Justin, McGee and Williams (1984) found that seven-year-olds who had language impairments scored significantly lower than other seven-year-olds on *non-verbal* scales, as well as on verbal scales and on the full scale of an intelligence test. In a similar vein, Stevenson and Richman (1976) found that 37 per cent of the three-year-olds in their study who had severely delayed expressive language also had comparable delays in their non-verbal intelligence.

Although the evidence indicates that low IQs are more common amongst children with language impairments than amongst the general population, it also indicates that most of the children who have a language impairment do not have a low IQ. For example, in Silva *et al.*'s study (1984), a sizeable proportion of the language impaired children (43%) had IQs of less than 90, but the majority (57%) had IQs of 90 or above, and 10 per cent of the children had IQs above 110. Thus, it is evident that language impairments can occur in children who have below average, average or above average intelligence.

3.6 Behaviour Problems

In the Dundee study (Drillien and Drummond, 1983), 26 per cent of the preschool children who had language disorders also had behaviour disorders (such as overactivity, poor concentration, attention seeking, tantrums, aggression, or negative and disruptive behaviour). This compares with an estimated frequency of 5.4 per cent for behaviour disorders in the total preschool population studied. Comparisons between the group of children who had language disorders alone and those who had both language and behaviour disorders revealed that the behaviourally disordered children typically had more severe expressive delay and were more likely to be clumsy.

Similar findings were obtained in Silva *et al.*'s study (1984) of seven-year-olds. The children who had language impairments had significantly more behaviour problems than other seven-year-olds. Furthermore, behaviour problems were particularly prevalent amongst those children who had a low IQ in addition to their language impairment, and these children also performed worse than other children on tests of motor ability.

3.7 Overview and Implications

Estimates of the prevalence of language impairments have varied between about 3 per cent and 15 per cent, depending on such factors as how language impairment is defined and how a sample of subjects is obtained. Prevalence rates are generally higher for boys and for children from lower socio-economic status backgrounds. While some children have problems which are fairly specific to language, other children's language disorders are accompanied by additional problems, such as low IQ, poor motor skills and behaviour disorders. The nature of causal relationships among these different problems is unclear. In particular, it is unclear whether SLI children whose IQs are within the normal range may nevertheless tend to have lower IQ scores than children with normal language development. A study conducted by Haynes and Naidoo (1991) of children attending a special school sheds some light on this issue. Although most of the children could be regarded as having a specific language impairment, they tended also to have a variety of other problems, for example in visuo-spatial, motor and behavioural areas. Unfortunately, direct comparisons with a normally developing control group were not carried out, but comparisons with previous studies suggested that such problems were more prevalent in the language impaired children than in the general population. Overall then, the findings reviewed in this chapter imply that different types of problems may sometimes cluster together and produce multiple difficulties for individual children. It is important to bear this in mind when planning assessment and intervention for children with language impairments.

CHAPTER 4

Prognosis for Children with Language Impairments

Despite the dearth of studies investigating the overall prevalence of language impairments in school age children, several researchers have conducted longitudinal studies in which children are followed up from the preschool period to various ages during the school period. The aim of these studies is to assess the subsequent development of children who had language impairments during their early years.

4.1 Stability of Language Impairments

An obvious first question regarding prognosis is whether the language impairments themselves are persistent or transient. Silva *et al.* (1983) found that 40 per cent of the children who had a language impairment at three years still had one at five years, and that 31 per cent of the children who had a language impairment at five years still had one at seven years. Compared to specific language impairments, general language impairments were more stable, persisting to age five for 79 per cent of the children who had a general language impairment at age three and persisting to age seven for 53 per cent of the children who had such an impairment at age five. Nevertheless, Silva *et al.*'s data indicate that there is also a fair degree of change across time. These changes operate in both directions: some children recover from an early disorder and other children have later disorders in their language development despite having progressed apparently normally at an earlier age. Consequently, Silva *et al.* stress the importance of assessing children's language at several points in their development.

There is also evidence that language problems can persist into adolescence. For example, in the National Child Development Study, 51 per cent of the children who had speech problems at seven years still had residual speech problems at sixteen years (Sheridan and Peckham, 1978). An even higher level of persistence was reported by Aram, Ekelman and Nation (1984) in a follow up study of a small sample of 20 children who had shown language problems at initial testing (when their ages ranged from 3 years 5 months to 6 years 11 months). When these children were tested ten years later, 70 per cent of them obtained low scores on a language test.

Studies of children with language impairments which have included follow-ups into adulthood are as yet comparatively rare. On the basis of findings from a follow-up study into adult life of boys with a severe and specific receptive language disorder, Rutter and Mawhood (1991) conclude that most of the children continued to show some language problems as adults (such as abnormal articulation or prosody, limited receptive vocabulary or poor conversational skills). Similarly, Haynes and Naidoo (1991) found that most of the ex-pupils from Dawn House (a special school for children with severe and specific language impairments) whom they followed up into early adulthood were judged, by themselves or their parents, as still having some problems with language. It should be noted, though, that both of these recent studies were restricted to individuals with initially severe language impairments and that they did not include a comparison group of individuals who had not been classed as language impaired in childhood.

An important issue raised by all these findings is whether it is possible to predict which children will recover from their language problems. Bishop and Edmundson (1987) found that assessments of four-year-old children who were referred to speech therapists could be used to predict with 90 per cent accuracy whether or not the problem would have resolved within 18 months. The children who were least likely to recover were those who had the most severe and most general impairments, as assessed by a battery of linguistic and non-linguistic tests. The best single predictor of outcome was the child's performance on the Bus Story Test (Renfrew, 1969), which requires the child to tell back a simple story about a set of pictures. The better children performed on this task at age four, the more likely they were to recover from their language problem by the time they were five years six months – perhaps because the task demanded a combination of phonological, syntactic, semantic and cognitive skills and hence assessed the breadth as well as the severity of a child's language impairment. The children who were most likely of all to recover were those who had a specific phonological impairment: 78 per cent of these children had a good outcome. A similar conclusion was drawn by Haynes and Naidoo (1991) on the basis of their detailed longitudinal study of pupils attending Dawn House. Phonological problems tended to be less persistent (and less severe) than semantic and syntactic ones.

The principle that general impairments resolve less readily than specific impairments applies not only to the number of aspects of language functioning which are affected, but also to whether the impairment extends to non-linguistic aspects of cognitive functioning. Bishop and Edmundson found that language problems resolved for 44 per cent of children with non-verbal intelligence within the normal range, but for only 11 per cent of children with low non-verbal intelligence. Similarly, Aram *et al.* (1984) found non-verbal intelligence to be a good predictor of whether language problems were resolved within the wider time span of ten years which they considered in their study.

One difficulty in assessing the stability of language impairments is that they may have different manifestations at different stages in a child's development. In addition, an initial language disorder may give rise to other problems (for example, behavioural ones) which may then persist even after the language impairment has resolved. For these reasons, it is important to consider subsequent developments in areas other than spoken language.

4.2 Prognosis for Reading Abilities

When Silva *et al.* (1987) followed up at ages seven, nine and eleven years those children who had had a language impairment at three years, they found that these children made significantly slower progress in learning to read than children who had not had a preschool language impairment. Reading problems were particularly evident and persistent for the group of children who had had a general language impairment at three years, as compared to those who had had a comprehension impairment only or an expressive impairment only. At ages seven and nine years, low reading scores were significantly more frequent for all three groups of children who had had a language impairment than for other children; but by age eleven years, it was only in the general language impairment group that children with low reading scores were over-represented.

Similar evidence of an increased incidence of reading problems amongst children with preschool language problems has emerged from follow ups at six years six months to seven years six months in the Dundee study (Drillien and Drummond, 1983), at seven years in the Newcastle study (Fundudis *et al.* 1979) and at eight years in the Waltham Forest study (Stevenson, 1984).

However, in a follow-up study at the age of about eight years six months of children who had had a language impairment at four years, Bishop and Adams (1990) found that it was only those children who had persistent problems with spoken language who were at increased risk of experiencing difficulties with literacy. Those children whose difficulties with spoken language had resolved by the age of about five years six months did not usually have any more difficulty than other children in learning to read and write. Furthermore, Bishop and Adams' results indicate that the reading problems which did occur (usually in children who had persisting problems with spoken language) were more likely to involve poor comprehension of the meaning of a passage than to involve difficulty in decoding individual words accurately.

4.3 Prognosis for Intelligence

The findings for intelligence are similar to those for reading. Once again, the most detailed picture is provided by Silva *et al.*'s study (1987). For all three groups of children who had had a language impairment at three years (whether general, receptive or expressive), there were significantly more children with low IQ scores at seven and at nine years than there were for children without a preschool language impairment. This applied to performance IQ as well as to verbal IQ and full-scale IQ. At eleven years of age, only the group who had had a general language impairment at three years continued to be over-represented amongst children with low performance IQ scores. On the other hand, for verbal IQ and full-scale IQ, all three types of language impaired group were still at a disadvantage by the age of eleven years.

These findings are compatible with those obtained in the Newcastle study (Fundudis *et al.* 1979) and the Waltham Forest study

(Stevenson, 1984) from follow ups at seven and eight years of age, respectively. In all three studies, the language impaired children were significantly more likely than other children to have low IQs. This held for verbal, performance and full-scale IQ but, as one would expect, it held most strongly for verbal IQ and least strongly for performance IQ.

4.4 Prognosis for Socio-Emotional and Behaviour Problems

Several studies have presented evidence suggesting that children with language impairments have an increased risk of experiencing socio-emotional or behaviour problems. A wide range of such problems has been reported, including difficulties in forming/maintaining social relationships, anxiety disorders, attention deficits, antisocial behaviour, aggressive behaviour, temper tantrums and disobedience.

The Newcastle, Waltham Forest and Dunedin studies all revealed trends towards socio-emotional/behavioural problems being more prevalent in primary school age children who had had a preschool language impairment than in other children. However, in the Dunedin study this applied only to the groups with a general language disorder or a comprehension disorder, and not to the group with an expressive language disorder (Silva *et al.* 1987). Furthermore, in the Waltham Forest study it was found that while the behavioural deviance rate of 45 per cent for the language impaired group was greater than the rate of 22 per cent for the overall sample of eight-year-olds, it was comparable to the behavioural deviance rate of 48 per cent which was obtained for a matched control group of eight-year-olds who had had behaviour problems without language problems when they were three years old. Consequently, Stevenson (1984) concludes that the link between early and later behaviour problems is probably more direct than the link between early language problems and later behaviour problems. On the other hand, some studies have suggested that the incidence of anxiety, attentional and social relationship problems tends to increase as people with language impairments grow older (Cantwell, Baker, Rutter, and Mawhood, 1989; Rutter and Mawhood, 1991).

4.5 Overview and Implications

Overall, the evidence from several longitudinal studies combines to indicate that children who have language problems during the preschool years are at increased risk of having reading problems, low IQ and socio-emotional/behaviour problems after starting school. This risk appears to be greatest for general language impairments, which in turn tend to be more stable than impairments which are specific to comprehension or to production.

Many questions remain to be answered regarding the nature and direction of causal links amongst the various problems. For example, is low IQ in school age children a result of earlier language problems or does it simply reflect stability in the children's IQs from pre-school to school? Are reading problems directly caused by problems with spoken language or is the association between these two problems attributable to their common link with low IQ? It is likely that the answers to such questions will prove to be complex and will reveal networks of causally related factors which vary in their relative influence from child to child. In an attempt to tease out some of the relationships amongst variables, Silva *et al.* (1987) re-analysed their results for IQ and reading test scores while controlling for the effects of the child's sex and level of social disadvantage. They found that the associations between preschool language problems and later low scores on IQ and reading tests still held, although less strongly than before. In other words, the link between language problems and low IQ (or between language problems and reading problems) was partly, but by no means wholly, attributable to both problems being more prevalent in boys and in socially disadvantaged children.

It is important to realize that although, as a group, children with preschool language problems were found to be at risk of later problems, a sizeable proportion of these children did not experience later problems. It would be useful to discover more about the factors influencing whether and to what extent individual children avoid later problems. A particularly unfortunate limitation in the longitudinal studies reviewed here is that they do not provide evidence on how variations in outcome were related to the amount and type of intervention the children received. Bishop and Edmundson (1987) did attempt to obtain such data, but because the effects of the initial severity of the language impairment were so strong and because therapy was most likely to be given to the children with the most severe impairments, they were unable to obtain conclusive results regarding the impact of therapy.

In summary, the available evidence indicates that children who have preschool language impairments constitute a vulnerable group, although it is less clear to what extent their vulnerability is directly attributable to their language impairments *per se*. This implies that approaches to assessment and intervention should be sufficiently flexible and wide-ranging to tackle a variety of intellectual, socio-emotional and behavioural problems, rather than focusing exclusively on language impairments.

CHAPTER 5

Assessing Language Disorders

As we have seen, language impairments are often associated with a variety of other disorders. Therefore, the assessment of children with language impairments frequently involves assessing a wide range of other abilities and characteristics in addition to language abilities. This, in turn, emphasizes the importance of a multi-disciplinary approach to assessment, in which there is collaboration amongst parents and different professionals, such as teachers, speech and language therapists, psychologists, psychiatrists, paediatricians and audiologists. In this chapter we will focus specifically on the assessment of language abilities, while remembering that in practice this would usually be only one part of a child's overall assessment.

5.1 Functions of Assessment

Several different functions of assessment can be distinguished:

(1) **identifying** whether a child has a language impairment;

(2) **diagnosing** the nature of the impairment;

(3) **planning intervention,** in terms of the goals to be tackled and the procedures for doing so;

(4) **monitoring** a child's progress during intervention;

(5) trying to determine a child's **prognosis**.

All these functions are important but, as Lahey (1988, 1990) amongst others has argued, they require different approaches to assessment. For example, the aim of identifying children with language impairments is usually best served by comparing the language performance of different children using norm-referenced standardized tests (see section 1.5). Such tests, though, are not particularly useful in planning intervention, since they tend not to provide sufficiently detailed information about the relevant aspects of the child's linguistic abilities. Criterion-referenced approaches to intervention are usually more appropriate when the aim is to plan intervention.

5.2 Contexts of Assessment

Lahey (1988) proposes a continuum of contexts in which language impairments can be assessed, ranging from standardized testing at one extreme to naturalistic observation at the other, with non-stand-ardized elicitation techniques at an intermediate point on the continuum. These contexts differ in terms of the amount of structure which is imposed by the person carrying out the assessment. Standardized testing imposes a high degree of structure, in that the tester follows a standard procedure for administering a pre-determined set of items so that the child's performance can be readily compared to that of a representative sample of other children. In contrast, naturalistic observation of the way children use and understand language in everyday contexts involves a much lower degree of structure. Non-standardized elicitation techniques are used to probe particular aspoects of the child's linguistic knowledge, often within a semi-naturalistic context. The different contexts are useful for obtaining different types of information, so it is usually advisable to assess a child's language abilities in a variety of contexts. One way of combining the different forms of assessment is to begin with standardized tests in order to establish whether the child has a language impairment, and then to use naturalistic observation to start building up a more detailed picture of the nature of the child's problems. Even more detail can be added to the picture by using non-standardized elicitation techniques to explore some of the hypotheses emerging from the naturalistic observations. Some examples of the specific assessment tools available within each context will now be considered.

5.3 Standardized Tests

These tests are useful for making comparisons between children because they provide information about how children of a particular age perform and because they include detailed, specific instructions about how the test should be administered (which is helpful in achieving consistency across testers and across children). There are three sub-categories of standardized tests which are commonly used in assessing children with language impairments, namely intelligence tests, tests of general language ability and tests of specific aspects of language ability.

Intelligence tests, such as the Wechsler Intelligence Scale for Children (WISC) and the British Ability Scales (BAS), provide a useful means of comparing children's linguistic ability with other aspects of their intellectual ability. For example, the WISC (Weschler, 1974) consists of a verbal scale and a performance scale, so a child's verbal IQ can be compared to her/his performance (or non-verbal) IQ as well as to her/his overall IQ. However, as Muller, Munro and Code (1981) point out, the WISC verbal scale does not provide a particularly comprehensive assessment of language abilities, in that it focuses mainly on vocabulary and comprehension. Furthermore, in a study of children with specific language impairments, Howlin and Kendall (1991) found that children's verbal IQ as measured on the WISC did not correlate highly with their scores on a range of more specialized language tests. The British Ability Scales (Elliot, Murray and Pearson, 1978) tap a wider range of linguistic skills than the WISC (e.g., they assess both comprehension and production of sentences), but still not in sufficient detail to provide much guidance regarding intervention. Another limitation of intelligence tests is that they may fail to identify some of the children who have language impairments, especially those whose difficulties are mainly expressive phonological and/or syntactic ones.

Tests of general language ability include the Reynell Developmental Language Scales (RDLS), which is probably the most commonly used test of this type in the UK. The RDLS (Reynell, 1979) provide separate assessments of receptive and expressive abilities for children between the ages of six months and six years. There are two versions of the Verbal Comprehension Scale, one of which is specially designed for children who have no speech, or poor motor control, or who are very shy, in that responses can be made non-verbally using a variety of simple motor movements. The RDLS is useful in comparing a child's comprehension and production skills, and since it assesses a wider range of linguistic skills than intelligence tests do, it provides a more representative assessment of a child's level of language ability. Nevertheless, precision is still lacking in relation to the specific aspects of language which pose problems for a particular child. For instance, when a child fails on a comprehension item it is often unclear which part (or parts) of the sentence he or she has failed to understand.

Tests of specific aspects of language ability are designed to provide more detailed assessments of a child's strengths and weaknesses in a particular area, such as phonology, vocabulary or syntax. For example, the Edinburgh Articulation Test (EAT) aims to assess the ability of three- to six-year-old children to produce consonant sounds in various positions in a word (Anthony, Bogle, Ingram, and McIsaac, 1971). Although this test can be useful in establishing the extent to which a child has an articulation problem, the number of speech sounds tested is not sufficiently large to yield a precise description of the nature of the problem (Muller *et al.* 1981). Also, the EAT focuses on articulation ability rather than phonological ability, since it does not provide much information about the extent to which a child can use sound contrasts to convey meaning contrasts (Grunwell, 1975).

Children's grammatical abilities can be assessed using the Test of Reception of Grammar (TROG) (Bishop, 1983). Again this test is limited to assessing comprehension (and not production), but it does enable the tester to obtain a relatively detailed picture of a child's ability to understand various grammatical structures (such as relative clauses, plurals and negatives). It can be used with children between the ages of four and thirteen years.

An example of a test used in assessing semantic abilities is the British Picture Vocabulary Scale (BPVS) in which children between the ages of three and eighteen years are asked to point to pictures to demonstrate their comprehension of word meanings (Dunn,

Dunn, Whetton, and Pintillie, 1982). An obvious restriction in this test is that it assesses receptive vocabulary only and not expressive vocabulary. Also, the information which it yields is essentially quantitative (concerning the size of a child's vocabulary) rather than qualitative, in that it does not reveal much about what children think particular words mean.

There are as yet very few standardized tests of pragmatic abilities, due partly to the fact that pragmatic development and disabilities are still very under-researched and poorly understood. Just about the only such test is Shulman's Test of Pragmatic Skills (Shulman, 1985), which was developed in the USA and is more widely used there than in the UK. The tester uses a standard set of probes within several play contexts (such as playing with puppets) to assess the child's ability to express a range of communicative intentions (such as requesting information, providing information or denying an assertion). The child's score can then be compared to normative developmental data. Although this test provides a useful starting point in a very difficult and uncharted area of assessment, its scope is limited to communicative intentions and it is unclear how these relate to other types of discourse skills. Also, the scoring system has been criticized for being too simplistic and for leaving too many judgements to the tester's interpretation (McTear and Conti-Ramsden, 1992).

5.4 Naturalistic Observations

Naturalistic observations either may be **reported** (for example by parents) to the person making the assessment or may be **direct** in the sense that they are made by the person conducting the assessment. In both cases, the observations are usually made either in an everyday setting (such as the child's home or classroom), or in a setting designed to mimic an everyday context as closely as possible (for example, a playroom in a clinic). Of course, the contexts which children encounter in everyday life vary in their familiarity, formality and degree of structure, so it is often useful to observe a child's behaviour in more than one type of context. The observer may either take on the role of a bystander or may interact with the child, in which case the aim will be to behave in as natural a way as possible.

Methods of eliciting reported observations of a child's language or communication include structured or unstructured interviews, checklists and scales. An important advantage of parental reports is that parents have usually observed their children in a wide variety of contexts over long periods of time and so their observations are likely to be more representative than those which could be made by a professional. On the other hand, there are of course potential problems relating to the reliability of retrospective reports and the extent to which objectivity can be maintained. Rutter (1987) argues that it is often possible to gain much valuable information about a child's linguistic and communicative abilities from an interview with parents, so long as the questions asked encourage the parents to provide specific examples of the evidence they have used in drawing their conclusions. Similar conclusions have come from studies evaluating the usefulness of parental checklists, which provide a more structured (and less labour intensive) means of obtaining information on children's linguistic and communicative behaviours (Bates, Bretherton and Snyder, 1988; Dale, Bates, Reznick, and Morisset, 1989; Rescorla, 1989; Camaioni, Castelli, Longobardi, and Volterra, 1991; Rescorla, Hadicke-Wiley and Escarce, 1993). Most of these studies have focused on children between the ages of about one and three years; the checklists have included assessments of the children's vocabulary, their ability to combine words and their ability to perform particular communicative acts either non-verbally or verbally (e.g. requesting food by pointing or by using words referring to food).

The consensus which emerges from these studies is that parental checklists yield accurate and reliable assessments of children's communicative and linguistic behaviours provided that parents are asked to make judgements about specific, current behaviours (rather than being asked to make global or retrospective judgements) and to give specific examples of their children's behaviours. Parental report instruments are particularly valuable in screening large numbers of children for possible language difficulties (Rescorla *et al.* 1993). However, when it is suspected that a particular child may have a language impairment, parental reports are probably best regarded as being complementary to other types of assessment.

The assessment of pragmatic disorders is an area in which checklists have become particularly popular recently (McTear and Conti-Ramsden, 1992). An example is the Pragmatics Profile of Early Communication Skills (Dewart and Summers, 1988) which is designed to be completed by clinicians on the basis of informal interviews with parents. Its scope is broader than that of the Test of Pragmatic Skills: as well as assessing communicative intentions, it also assesses the child's responses to communicative acts, various interactive aspects of the child's ability (such as how the child initiates and maintains communicative exchanges) and how the child's communicative abilities vary across contexts. The Pragmatics Profile provides specific descriptions and examples of communicative behaviour and includes information about developmental sequences. However, since it is based on normal pragmatic development, it may fail to detect some abnormal features of pragmatic development (Letts and Reid, 1994).

Behaviour checklists are sometimes also used by professionals in conducting direct observations of children's linguistic and communicative abilities, although these will often be supplemented by more detailed linguistic analyses of a sample of the child's language.

In order to obtain a language sample, the clinician will typically select or set up contexts which are likely to encourage the child to talk. For example, a set of toys or pictures may be used to engage the child in conversation. The session is recorded on audio-tape or video-tape for later transcription and analysis. Crystal, Fletcher and Garman (1976) recommend that 30 minutes of conversation should be recorded, with half of this being about the immediate context and the other half about situations other than the 'here and now'. The way the language sample is analysed will depend partly on the aspects of language which are posing problems for a particular child. In recent years, several procedures have been devised for analysing samples of spontaneous language to obtain profiles of a child's strengths and weaknesses in particular areas of language.

One of the best known of these procedures is the Language Analysis, Remediation and Screening Procedure (LARSP), developed by Crystal, Fletcher and Garman (1976). This is a tool for producing a detailed profile of the grammatical characteristics of a child's language. It includes a profile chart which outlines various grammatical structures typical of children at particular stages of normal language development. Analysis involves determining which of these structures are used in the child's speech and which structures pose problems for the child. Since the profile chart arranges grammatical structures according to their developmental sequence, it provides guidelines regarding the order in which structures should be targeted in remediation.

Crystal (1982) also developed a Profile of Phonology (PROPH), a Prosody Profile (PROP) and a Profile in Semantics (PRISM). PROPH requires a sample of about 100 words of connected speech. These are analysed in terms of the speech sounds which the child produces correctly, the nature of errors, and the occurrence of phonological processes. PROP focuses mainly on intonation, but it can also be used to describe other prosodic features, such as the speed and rhythm of speech. PRISM consists of two sub-procedures: PRISM-L, which is used in analysing the child's vocabulary or lexicon, and PRISM-G, which is used in analysing the way meaning is conveyed by grammatical elements of a sentence. In order to apply PRISM, it is necessary to obtain several language samples relating to different topics of conversation and hence calling for different types of vocabulary.

As yet, there are no fully-developed linguistic profiling tools for pragmatic abilities, although there are a few promising illustrations of how the linguistic profiling approach can be applied to the assessment of children with pragmatic disorders (Adams and Bishop, 1989; Bishop and Adams, 1989; Letts and Reid, 1994).

One of the main advantages of profiles of the type developed by Crystal and his colleagues is that they result in descriptions of a child's abilities and problems which are sufficiently detailed to be useful in planning goals for intervention and in monitoring the child's progress during intervention. Also, since these assessment tools are applied to language produced in naturalistic situations, they have high ecological validity (that is, the conclusions drawn are likely to be relevant to the child's ability to use language in everyday life). On the more negative side, collecting, transcribing and analysing a language sample is much more time-consuming than administering and scoring a standardized test. Furthermore, a relatively high degree of technical expertise in linguistics is required in order to complete the profiles. Assessment techniques based on naturalistic observations tend to focus more on expressive abilities than on receptive abilities, because of the difficulty of determining how far a child's comprehension is based on linguistic as opposed to non-linguistic cues. There can also be problems (though usually less severe ones) in interpreting children's language production in naturalistic situations. For example, if a child fails to produce a particular grammatical structure, it is not always clear whether she is incapable of doing so or whether she has simply not used it in the particular context sampled. Therefore, it is often helpful to probe a child's areas of apparent weakness in more depth by following up naturalistic observations with non-standardized elicitation techniques, such as those described in the next section.

5.5 Non-Standardized Elicitations

Non-standardized elicitations are techniques which impose more structure on the assessment situation than naturalistic observation techniques do, with the aim of encouraging children to produce particular linguistic forms if these are in their repertoire. In this way, it should be possible to resolve some of the interpretation problems arising from naturalistic observations and hence to obtain a clearer picture of where a child's difficulties lie.

Since the particular elicitation techniques used will depend on the specific issues to be addressed, which in turn will depend on the pattern of performance shown by the individual child in previous assessments, clinicians usually either devise their own techniques or adapt research techniques from the child language literature (Lahey, 1988). Consequently, a wide variety of elicitation techniques are in use. Examples of the types of techniques used include sentence completion tasks, asking the child to answer questions about pictures or stories, and asking the child to describe a scenario enacted with puppets or other toys. Non-standardized techniques can also be used to assess a child's comprehension, for instance by asking the child to enact sentences produced by the tester.

Non-standardized elicitations represent a compromise between naturalistic observation and standardized testing. As such, they share some of the advantages and some of the disadvantages of each of these types of assessment, although usually in a less extreme form.

5.6 Overview and Implications

It is clear from research with children whose language is developing normally that different research techniques will often yield different (and sometimes conflicting) pictures of a child's linguistic abilities, and that the relationship between comprehension and production in language development is not always straightforward (Bloom, 1974; Clark and Hecht, 1983; Donaldson, 1986; Donaldson and Laing, 1993). Therefore, it is important to investigate children's language abilities in a range of different contexts. The preceding discussion indicates that this point applies equally, if not even more strongly, to the assessment of children who have language disorders. For example, when Howlin and Kendall (1991) tested a group of children attending a Language Unit on a range of commonly used language tests, they found that there were large discrepancies between the scores obtained on different tasks by the same children. Consequently, Howlin and Kendall emphasize the need to build up a profile of the child's language skills by using a variety of assessment procedures which involve both structured and natural-istic settings and which tap different aspects of the child's language use and processing abilities. Similarly, Stackhouse and Wells (1993) present a case study of a child with a severe speech disorder to highlight the value of using a combination of types of assessments (including standardized tests, linguistic analyses of spontaneous speech samples, specially designed tasks and tasks derived from the research literature) to test out hypotheses about the specific nature of an individual child's difficulties and hence to construct a psy-cholinguistic profile of her or his strengths and weaknesses. Such a profile, in turn, provides a sound basis for planning appropriate intervention.

CHAPTER 6

Approaches to Intervention

6.1 Issues of Intervention

An important issue in working with children who have language difficulties is how professionals and parents can most effectively enhance or improve the children's ability to communicate. To be effective, intervention strategies must be geared to the needs of the individual child and therefore must be closely integrated with thorough, ongoing assessment procedures. Few would disagree with this statement, although there is less agreement about exactly how information from diagnostic assessments should be translated into intervention strategies. For example, should the main aim be to develop a child's strengths so as to compensate for his/her weaknesses, or should the emphasis be on developing the skills in which he/she is weakest? Whatever the answer to this question, it is clear that the more general question of 'What is the best intervention strategy for language disorders?' is highly unlikely to be answerable in such a simple form. Instead, we need to ask a series of more specific and more complex questions concerning the effectiveness of particular intervention techniques in achieving particular goals, for particular types of children, with particular types of language disorders, in particular sets of circumstances. The following sections aim to illustrate the range of possible approaches to intervention for children with language disorders and to consider some of the evidence which can be used in addressing questions of effectiveness.

Intervention strategies vary along several dimensions, corresponding to the following questions:

(1) **What** should be taught or developed?

(2) **How** should the intervention be carried out?

(3) **Who** should carry out the intervention?

(4) **Where** should the intervention take place?

In other words, there is variation in the goals of intervention, in the techniques used to achieve these goals, in the agents who implement the techniques, and in the settings where the intervention takes place.

6.2 Goals of Intervention

An intervention will usually have a variety of goals, ranging from very general goals to more specific goals or objectives. Typically, goals are arrived at through assessment procedures which are rather different from those through which the initial diagnosis of a particular language or communication disorder was made. Assessment for the purposes of diagnosis will probably be made using norm-referenced, standardized tests, which involve comparing the child's performance with that of a representative sample of other (usually normally-developing) children and the assignation of an age-equivalent or other standardized score. Such norm-referenced assessments are not usually sufficiently detailed or informative for the purposes of planning intervention. For this purpose, clinicians may turn to criterion-referenced procedures, in which the child's performance is compared to a more detailed set of criteria or goals. These are typically organized as developmentally-sequenced levels, and the child's abilities are matched to a developmental level or other standard, either through observation or through testing (which may be informal or standardized). Examples of assessments used for planning treatment would be the Detailed Test of Comprehension, from the Derbyshire Language Scheme (Knowles and Masidlover, 1982) which is an unstandardized test, and the Pragmatics Profile (Dewart and Summers, 1988) in which information on developmental level is gained through a structured interview with the child's parents or carers. Linguistic profiles (Crystal, 1982) derived through the analysis of elicited speech samples can also be useful in identifying goals of intervention, particularly for children who have more complex and persisting impairments and who are receiving intensive remediation, for example in a language unit.

Assessment procedures will often give rise to a number of possible goals of intervention, thus requiring an order of priority to be established. The literature on language development in normal children can sometimes be used as a basis for selecting 'developmental' goals, so that the child can be helped to achieve those aspects of language which would be the next to appear according to some generally agreed developmental sequence. This approach works rather better for those aspects of language about which there is a large literature, such as the acquisition of grammatical tense inflections, but can be problematic in areas about which less developmental information is available, such as the acquisition of conversational rules. In fact, developmental goals may not be particularly functionally relevant to a given child in her/his own circumstances. The selection of appropriate goals may therefore be influenced by functional considerations, so that the language skills acquired suit the individual needs of the child and are more likely to lead to pragmatic gains.

Although different types of intervention goals are far from mutually exclusive, there has been a historical shift away from an emphasis on the structure of language towards an emphasis on language as a tool for communication. The relative emphasis on these two types of goal also varies according to the nature of a child's language problems. For instance, for a child with a phonological-syntactic disorder, intervention is likely to focus on language form, although not in isolation from function, whereas for a child with a semantic-pragmatic disorder, intervention is more likely to focus on the communicative functions of language, although not in isolation from the linguistic tools required to achieve communicative goals.

At a more specific level, intervention may target phonological, syntactic, semantic or pragmatic aspects of a child's language, or non-linguistic skills which are felt to provide some of the relevant underpinnings for more efficient language learning, such as attention to sound, turn-taking, representational play or matching and sorting. Within each of these aspects even more specific goals will usually be formulated to guide intervention (Fey, 1986; Harris, 1990; Lees and Urwin, 1991).

When a child has no speech or only very limited speech, a decision has to be taken as to whether the goals of intervention should include the introduction of an alternative or augmentative communication system to serve in place of or supplement the use of spoken language. Alternative or augmentative communication systems include manual sign languages (such as British Sign Language), more limited systems of manual signs (such as Makaton which uses a vocabulary of signs derived from British Sign Language), symbol systems (such as Blissymbolics and the Rebus system), pictorial systems and written language. Recent advances in micro-computer technology have greatly enhanced the power and flexibility of alternative/augmentative communication systems. For example, so long as children have the ability to make at least one voluntary movement and hence to control an electronic switch or a cursor on a computer screen, computers can be used to present them with menus of options from which they can make choices to construct and communicate messages. The output from electronic communication aids can take various forms, such as symbols or written language presented on a computer screen, or synthesized speech.

Resistance to the introduction of alternative or augmentative communication systems sometimes occurs on the grounds that they are stigmatizing, do not significantly help to reduce social isolation and may prevent the development of spoken language. There is little evidence to support the last of these points. The input to users of alternative or augmentative communication systems typically consists of signs or symbols presented along with speech (either natural or synthesized). Kiernan (1987) reports that children who receive augmentative communication programmes have frequently been found to develop the ability to vocalize and to produce speech.

Decisions about which particular augmentative communication system to introduce can also be contentious, and are likely to be influenced by the relative weightings given to such factors as ease of learning, flexibility of the system as a communication tool, the number and availability of people able to use the system, and cost. For example, symbol systems tend to be easier to learn than sign systems, perhaps because recall memory is required in order to produce the appropriate sign, whereas the appropriate symbol can be selected using only recognition memory (since the set of alternative symbols is usually laid out in front of the child). On the other hand, symbol systems are typically less flexible and powerful as communication tools (Kiernan, 1987; Howlin, 1989). The choice of an augmentative communication system also needs to take into account the characteristics of the individual child, such as his/her cognitive, perceptual and motor skills.

Similarly, the issue of what constitutes the most appropriate means of communication for children with hearing impairments has often been the subject of fierce and heated debate. Three main types of communication system can be distinguished:

oral languages (such as spoken English);

sign languages involving manual gestures (such as British Sign Language), which are languages in their own right, with grammatical systems which are distinct from other languages;

sign systems (such as signed English) in which manual gestures are used as analogues of English words and grammatical inflections.

As noted earlier (see section 2.4), deaf children who learn sign language as their first language from fluent signers show a comparable rate of development to that shown by hearing children acquiring spoken language. However, the majority of deaf children have hearing parents and not all deaf parents are fluent in sign language. In these cases, the factors governing decisions about which communication system or combination of systems should be used are complex and relate both to psycholinguistic issues and to social psychological issues (such as attitudes and group identity). Useful reviews of relevant evidence and arguments are provided by Quigley and Paul (1987) and by Messer (1994).

6.3 Intervention Techniques

A vast range of intervention techniques are used with children who have language disorders, since most clinicians devise individualized programmes based on the needs of the particular child, combined with their own experience of what has proved successful in the past. Nevertheless, these techniques can be grouped into three broad categories: behavioural approaches, naturalistic approaches and 'compromise' approaches.

Behavioural approaches to language intervention are based on the principles of learning theory and hence on the assumption that language can be learned through such processes as imitation, reinforcement, shaping, modelling and prompting. For example, if the goal is to teach a child to use personal pronouns (such as *he* and *she*) appropriately, exercises might be presented in which the child is shown a picture (e.g. of a girl swimming) and is asked a question (e.g. *What is the girl doing?*). The question could then be followed by a prompt (*Say 'she is swimming'*) to encourage the child to imitate the appropriate response. A correct imitation could then be reinforced by praising the child. Modelling is similar to imitation, but the child is not asked to reproduce the therapist's utterance immediately. Instead, the child is asked to listen carefully to the therapist producing utterances containing the linguistic forms which are the target of intervention. Then the child is given a turn at speaking in a context similar to the one in which the therapist has modelled the relevant linguistic forms. For instance, the therapist and child may take turns at describing a set of pictures.

There are a number of studies indicating that behavioural techniques can be effective in improving the production of various linguistic forms in children with a specific language disorder (Leonard, 1981). However, children often experience difficulties in generalizing what they have learned to related linguistic constructions. Hegde, Noll and Pecora (1979) taught children to use *is* in sentences beginning with *he* and found that although the children successfully generalized their use of *is* to other sentences beginning with *he*, they failed to generalize to sentences beginning with *she*. Problems can also arise in generalizing to situations which differ from the training situation. Leonard (1981) outlines four of the ways in which situations may differ from the training situation: in terms of the visual stimuli talked about (e.g. real situations versus pictures), in terms of the verbal stimuli used as prompts (e.g. open-ended versus explicit questions), in terms of the setting (e.g. home versus clinic), and in terms of the co-conversationalist (e.g. parent versus therapist). On the basis of several studies investigating generalization effects, Leonard concludes that use of a trained linguistic form is usually successfully generalized to situations which differ from the training situation in only one or two of these respects, but that problems in generalizing tend to arise when situations differ in three or four respects. It is therefore important for behavioural training to be conducted in a variety of contexts.

Similar generalization problems have been observed in intervention studies which have used structured tasks to develop more general skills, such as word-finding strategies. For example, Hyde Wright (1993) found that a training programme for children with word-finding problems was effective in improving their ability to name the pictures used during training and that there was some generalization to other pictures when these were presented in the therapy room. On the other hand, there was very little evidence of the children generalizing the strategies to situations outside the therapy room, even when these also involved picture naming.

Naturalistic approaches to language intervention are based on the assumption that children will learn language best in situations where it is being used to serve genuine communicative purposes and where it is closely integrated with real life activities. This assumption is often accompanied by the assumption that children's language problems can be resolved through incidental learning. Thus, the role of the therapist or teacher is not to improve the use of particular linguistic forms through explicit teaching, but rather to facilitate incidental learning of linguistic forms in meaningful communicative contexts by providing appropriate linguistic input and opportunities for the child to use the targeted linguistic behaviour. One way of making communicative contexts meaningful is to base them around activities and topics which are of interest to the child and which relate to her or his experiences. Therefore, naturalistic intervention programmes need to be tailored to the interests of individual children, as well as to their need for an emphasis on a particular type of linguistic input. Another way of ensuring that interventions occur in meaningful, relevant contexts is to carry them out within real-life settings, such as the classroom, playground or home, rather than withdrawing the child to a separate room or to a speech and language therapy clinic. This, in turn, encourages collaboration in the intervention process to occur with significant people in the child's life, such as parents, siblings, peers, class teachers and nursery nurses. (Of course, collaboration with at least some of these people can also be encouraged in a clinic setting, but in a more contrived way.) Advocates of naturalistic approaches include McLean and Snyder-McLean (1978), Harris (1988), Lahey (1988) and Watson (1990).

Since the naturalistic approach involves intervening either in everyday settings or in settings designed to mimic everyday settings, problems of generalizing what is learned from the therapeutic situation to real-life situations are avoided or substantially reduced. Bochner *et al.* (1980) present two case studies which highlight typical differences between the naturalistic approach and the more traditional behavioural approach. One five-year-old who had a language disorder and a suspected mild mental handicap received language intervention based on the behavioural approach, whereas another five-year-old who had similar problems received intervention based on the naturalistic approach. Both children made progress in language skills, but the nature of this progress differed between the two children. The child who had received behavioural intervention acquired the skills she had been drilled in, such as labelling pictures and objects and answering direct questions, but she did not succeed in generalizing these skills to normal conversations with her teachers and peers when she moved from a special education class into a mainstream class. In contrast, the child who had received the naturalistic intervention did acquire spontaneous language skills which generalized to the new setting of a mainstream class. Bochner *et al.* see their findings as evidence for the claim that 'children learn what they are taught' (1980: 100). Although this conclusion is based on a qualitative study of only two children, it is broadly consistent with the conclusion reached by Leonard (1981) on the basis of more extensive evidence (from a review of studies). He concludes that training which focuses only on particular linguistic forms tends to yield effects limited to the child's use of these forms, whereas training with a more general focus usually results in broader linguistic gains.

When considering issues of generalization, it is important to remember that the contexts in which children are likely to have to deploy linguistic skills are not restricted to low-structure, informal contexts in which language is closely linked to their own immediate purposes and concerns. It is true that such contexts predominate in the lives of young children, but if children are to progress successfully in the educational system, they will also have to cope with more formal contexts in which language is 'disembedded' from immediate purposes (Donaldson, 1978). In particular, the ability to use and understand language in disembedded contexts, and perhaps also to reflect on the formal properties of language, is likely to be crucial to the acquisition of literacy. Such considerations become especially significant in the light of the evidence indicating that children with spoken language disorders are at risk of encountering reading problems (Silva, 1987) (see section 4.2).

The naturalistic approach has considerable intuitive appeal since it is consistent with contemporary theories of normal language acquisition. Although such theories differ in whether they emphasize innate knowledge of the structural properties of language (e.g. Chomsky, 1986) or the acquisition of language within supportive social contexts (e.g. Bruner, 1983), they have in common an eschewal of the role of explicit language teaching by adults. However, despite the superficial plausibility of the argument that intervention procedures for children with language disorders should aim to mimic the processes by which language is normally acquired, some caution is called for. It does not necessarily follow that the 'normal' developmental route is the best route for all children. The very fact that children with language disorders have not made normal progress in acquiring language 'naturally' suggests that an alternative approach may be beneficial or even necessary.

Of course, most naturalistic intervention approaches are alternative approaches in the sense that they aim to adapt normal interactions to the child's needs, by for example providing extra opportunities to observe and practice linguistic forms or functions which are posing problems. However, as Conant, Budoff, Hecht, and Morse (1984) point out, a potential difficulty is that opportunities to work on particular problem areas may not arise sufficiently frequently in natural situations. Furthermore, considerable skill and ingenuity on the part of the teacher or therapist are required in order to exploit naturally occurring opportunities for intervention.

Compromise approaches aim to combine the advantages of traditional behavioural approaches with those of more naturalistic approaches. For example, Conant *et al.* (1984) devised an intervention programme consisting of a set of communication games in which particular features of syntax, vocabulary or articulation could be focused upon, but in which these features served the same pragmatic functions as in normal conversation. In these games, the roles of speaker and hearer were alternated between the child and the teacher. For example, hiding games were used in which the child and the teacher took turns at guessing where an object was hidden.

The materials for this game could be constructed in such a way as to encourage the use of particular linguistic forms in the guesses. The feedback which the child received related not to arbitrary standards of 'correctness' but to the communicative adequacy or inadequacy of his messages (e.g. whether the child succeeded in communicating his guess to the adult so that she could look for the object in the place the child had intended). Conant *et al.* found that children who received their intervention programme over a period of four months made more progress (in terms of the quality of their spontaneous speech) than an untreated control group. This effect applied to children whose language disorder was accompanied either by a moderate cognitive delay or by no cognitive delay. It did not hold for children who had a severe cognitive delay.

Conant *et al.*'s findings illustrate the effectiveness of compromise approaches to intervention. Similar approaches have been devised by several other authors. For instance, the Metaphon approach to treating phonological disorders (Howell and Dean, 1994) also employs communication games as a means of focusing intervention on particular phonological contrasts within pragmatically appropriate contexts. Recent efficacy studies of Metaphon have yielded encouraging results (Howell and Dean, 1994; Reid *et al.* in press).

Howlin (1987, 1989) reports that in recent years behavioural approaches to intervention have become less artificial and that behavioural techniques are now usually employed in communicatively meaningful contexts. She further suggests that the degree of structure which is appropriate in a language intervention approach will depend on characteristics of the child. In particular, she proposes that more highly structured programmes may be best suited to children with very limited linguistic skills or those with limited motivation to communicate (e.g. severely autistic children).

In summary, there is a general dearth of good research into the efficacy of interventions for children with language impairments (Vetter, 1991). Although many of the available intervention techniques have been shown to produce some positive effects, no particular technique stands out as being more effective overall than other techniques (Leonard, 1981; Nye, Foster and Seaman, 1987). The literature also suggests that different techniques produce different types of positive effects and that different techniques are probably appropriate for different types of children. However, clear and detailed evidence is lacking on which techniques are best suited to which children. In the circumstances, the best strategy is likely to be to adopt an approach to intervention which is eclectic and individualized, yet principled. Intervention goals and techniques should be closely integrated with thorough assessments of the individual child's strengths and weaknesses. Useful illustrations of this type of principled approach are provided by recently published case studies of a child with a speech disorder (Stackhouse and Wells, 1993) and of a child with a pragmatic disorder (Letts and Reid, 1994).

6.4 Agents of Intervention

Because of the varied nature of language disorders and the fact that they are often associated with other types of problems, a wide range of professionals can be involved in planning and implementing intervention for children with language disorders. Those most frequently involved are teachers, speech and language therapists and educational psychologists. Other professionals who are not infrequently involved include nursery nurses, classroom auxiliaries/assistants, speech and language therapy assistants, clinical psychologists, psychiatrists, paediatricians, nurses, audiologists, health visitors and social workers. Good communication and collaboration between different professionals is obviously of great importance but is not always easily achieved in practice, especially since three different service agencies are often involved (Education, Health and Social Work).

There is increasing recognition of the value of parents playing an active role in intervention. The rationale for this is partly related to arguments about the merits of naturalistic interventions, but also relates to the fact that parental involvement will usually increase the amount and continuity of the intervention which can be given to a child. Several studies have yielded evidence confirming the value of involving parents (to varying extents) in intervention (Lovaas, Koegel, Simmons, and Stevens, 1973; Ward and Kellett, 1982; Broen and Westman, 1990). An interesting recent study evaluated the efficacy of an intervention approach in which groups of parents received training from a speech and language therapist in techniques designed to help their children (who had expressive language delays) to progress from single-word to multi-word utterances (Gibbard, 1994). The findings indicated that the parental-based intervention was at least as effective as (and possibly slightly more effective than) direct therapy in which the therapist treated each child individually. Although Gibbard found that most parents were keen to participate, it is nevertheless important to be aware of the potential danger of imposing too many demands on parents (Howlin, 1987), and to recognize that parents' attitudes and circumstances will vary. Parental choice (e.g., regarding the type of role they prefer to play) is a vital element of parental involvement.

In discussing her findings, Gibbard argues that a parental-based group approach may be a more cost-effective model of service delivery than direct one-to-one therapy (delivered to the individual child by the speech and language therapist). This is consistent with a growing awareness amongst speech and language therapists of the value of considering alternative models of service delivery in order to provide effective intervention for as many clients as possible (Enderby and Davies, 1989; College of Speech and Language Therapists, 1991). Thus, in some circumstances, it may be appropriate for the therapist to act as a consultant or facilitator who delivers therapy indirectly by collaborating with parents, teachers, nursery nurses or other professionals. As yet, there has been very little systematic evaluation of the strengths and weaknesses of different models of service delivery for children with language impairments, although some research of this type is currently in progress (Grieve *et al.* forthcoming).

6.5 Settings of Intervention

Children with language disorders are to be found in a wide range of educational settings, such as mainstream nursery schools and schools, various types of special schools, and special classes or units (e.g., language units). In addition, preschool children with language disorders may be attending playgroups or nurseries (run privately or by the social work department), or they may not be receiving any form of preschool provision. Language intervention may take place within any of these settings or in a speech and language therapy clinic (either within or outwith one of these settings) or in the home. We will now look in some detail at the nature of the provision within one particular type of setting, namely language units.

Language Units

Language units are of particular interest in that they aim to cater specifically for children with language disorders and to promote collaboration amongst different types of professional, especially teachers, speech therapists and educational psychologists. Also, they represent a compromise between mainstream and special education.

Surveys of language units in Scotland (Working Party of Scottish Principal Educational Psychologists, 1988) and in Britain as a whole (Donlan, 1987) have revealed that language units vary considerably on a number of dimensions.

First, they vary in terms of the age range which they cater for. Some units cater for children of any age within the preschool and primary age range, whereas other units cater for only part of this age range. There are very few language units for secondary school age children in Britain.

Second, different language units have different admission criteria. In the Scottish survey, it was found that approximately half of the teachers (from the 12 units surveyed in detail) were able to give clearly defined admission criteria, whereas the other half said either that there were no rigid criteria or that they themselves were not directly involved in admission procedures. There were three criteria on which there was a clear consensus among staff from different units:

(1) a need for intensive speech therapy;

(2) mainstream children with specific language difficulties;

(3) exclusion of other major primary causes of failure to develop language (mental, physical, emotional or sensory).

However, when staff were asked (in another questionnaire) to describe the characteristics of the children who were actually attending their unit, 75 per cent of the children were described as having other significant difficulties, with 26 per cent of children being described as having 'cognitive difficulties resulting in generalized delay or learning difficulties' and 22 per cent as having 'social/emotional difficulties'. Of course, some of these other difficulties may have been secondary effects rather than primary causes of the children's linguistic difficulties. However, even allowing for this and for the fact that about 50 per cent of units were not able to state rigid admission criteria, it appears that there may sometimes be discrepancies between admission policy and admission practice. Similarly, Donlan (1987) reports that in his survey 32 per cent of units showed a discrepancy between the staff's descriptions of the children's problems and the stated admission criteria.

Furthermore, in relation to the specific criterion of normal non-verbal intelligence, Donlan (1987) writes:

> 'Of those stating criteria only 45 per cent included the requirement of non-verbal ability within the average range. Good practice in the longer established Units and Schools continues to emphasise the importance of establishing a deficit in verbal versus non-verbal levels of functioning. But present trends in Educational Psychology appear to be in dispute with this practice…' (p.47)

In a more recent study of children attending four language units in the North West of England, Conti-Ramsden, Donlan and Grove (1992) also found that the teachers stressed that the units' function was to cater for children with normal cognitive development, and yet two out of the fifteen children studied were discovered to have global delays (affecting their non-verbal cognitive abilities as well as their language abilities).

The argument that language unit admission should be restricted to children with **specific** language disorders is based partly on an underlying assumption that general cognitive development constrains linguistic development and therefore that children whose language problems are associated with a general cognitive delay are less likely to benefit from the interventions provided in language units. However, these assumptions are not entirely clearcut. There has been a historical shift in the theories which psycholinguists have postulated regarding relationships between cognitive and linguistic development. For example, Cromer originally advanced the Cognition Hypothesis which states that linguistic development is constrained by cognitive development, but he has since revised this to a much less extreme and more complex position in which he argues that linguistic abilities can sometimes develop far in advance of non-verbal intelligence (Cromer, 1991).

It is true that language problems have been found to resolve less readily for children with IQs below the normal range (see section 4.1), but this could be interpreted either as an argument for or against admitting such children to a language unit. Furthermore, when Cole, Dale and Mills (1990) compared a group of children who had cognitive skills markedly above their linguistic skills with a group whose cognitive and linguistic skills were similarly impaired, they found that both groups benefited from language intervention over a one year period. It is also important to recognize that research has so far failed to identify a single underlying cause for specific language impairment (SLI), that children with SLI probably do not themselves constitute a homogeneous group and that many of them do show various subtle non-linguistic difficulties, for example with auditory processing or symbolic play (Reid and Donaldson, 1993) (see section 2.5).

Another argument which may underlie all three of the admission criteria which were identified in the survey is that since language unit placement is a scarce and expensive resource, it should be targeted on those children for whom enhanced language skills would make unsupported mainstream education a realistic goal.

A third respect in which language units vary is in terms of their relationships to mainstream schools. Of the twelve units studied in detail in the Scottish survey, eight were situated in mainstream primary schools, one in a mainstream nursery school, two in child guidance clinics and one in a hospital. In most of the units attached to schools, opportunities for integration were limited to locational integration (being on the same site) and social integration (mixing socially at break times). A few of the units also had some functional integration in which the children from the language unit shared some educational activities with children from the mainstream part of the school. Only one unit tried to re-introduce children gradually to mainstream schooling before they returned to a mainstream school on a permanent, full-time basis. However, in half of the units catering for primary school age children, the children attended the unit only part time and most of them spent the rest of the school week in a mainstream school.

The nature of staffing also varies from unit to unit. The most usual pattern in the Scottish survey was for the full-time staff to be a teacher and a nursery nurse or auxiliary, with educational psychologists and speech and language therapists being part-time members of staff. However, one unit had a full-time speech and language therapist and another unit was run on the basis of part-time input from speech and language therapists without any input from teachers. Some units had one educational psychologist working in the unit on a regular basis, whereas other units had several psychologists participating as case workers. The latter arrangement was regarded as unsatisfactory both by the psychologists and by the teachers. Since most units were staffed by more than one type of professional, it appears superficially at least that there was an interdisciplinary approach to intervention. However, it was found that the week's activities were decided upon by a multidisciplinary team in only half the units. In the other units, this decision was made by the person in charge (who was usually a teacher).

As part of the survey, language unit staff were asked what they saw as their roles within the unit. The most frequently mentioned role for speech and language therapists was assessment, for psychologists it was involvement in future placement, for teachers it was group and class teaching, and for nursery nurses it was creating and supervising play experiences. However, each group also mentioned various other roles fairly frequently and there was some overlap between professions in these. For example, speech and language therapists, psychologists and teachers were all involved in assessment, reviews and devising individual intervention programmes. It is unclear, though, to what extent this overlap in roles is indicative of collaboration as opposed to duplication of effort or even conflict.

When the staff were asked how they would like their roles to change, it was found that the speech and language therapists and psychologists were the groups who most wanted changes. The speech and language therapists frequently expressed a desire to be more involved in working in the classroom, in collaboration with teachers and using a less formal approach to intervention. This is consistent with the increasing shift towards more naturalistic intervention approaches, as discussed in section 6.3. The psychologists typically wanted to spend more time in the unit working with the staff on communication approaches and they also wanted to work more with parents.

Parental involvement in the units was found to be very limited. The Working Party (1988) concluded that:

> 'In most units consideration was given to the concept of partnership, but little evidence of it occurred in practice. There was no evidence of parents taking an active part in decision-making processes.' (p.79)

In view of the evidence on the value of parental involvement (see section 6.4), this is clearly a matter for concern.

One of the most interesting aspects of the Scottish survey concerns the staff's perceptions of the advantages of the language unit. Answers to the question 'What does the unit have to offer to help children's language development?' showed a high degree of consistency across professions. The most frequent responses were 'a high staff ratio enabling individual and small group teaching' (given by 74% of respondents), 'understanding of the children's needs – a supportive environment' (52%), 'a curriculum geared to developing language and communication' (46%) and 'speech therapy provision' (46%). It is interesting to note that responses relating specifically to language came third in this list, which is perhaps surprising in the light of the emphasis given to specific language impairments in the criteria for admission to many language units. The characteristics of the units mentioned in the two most frequent responses are ones which are likely to be beneficial to any special needs child or indeed to any child. A related question asked staff to specify the approaches which they felt were most helpful to children's communication development. Once again, there was a considerable degree of consensus in responses to this question. The most frequent responses referred to games and free play, real life situations and child-centred approaches encouraging spontaneous child-initiated communication. This clearly indicates a commitment to naturalistic approaches to intervention (see section 6.3), although no evidence is provided on the extent to which this commitment was put into practice.

An important question is whether language units are effective in remediating children's language disorders, but unfortunately there are very few studies addressing this question. Urwin, Cook and Kelly (1988) followed up children who had attended a preschool language unit and whose ages at follow-up ranged from six to eleven years. They found that 84 per cent of the children were in main-stream schools. These children were judged by their teachers to be well-integrated members of their class and to have made progress over the previous 12 months. Urwin *et al.* report that the average verbal IQ and general IQ for the group at follow-up were in the low average range (89 and 94, respectively). However, in the absence of data on the children's scores before entry to the language unit and in the absence of a comparison group who had not attended a language unit, it is difficult to see what can be concluded about the effectiveness of language units from these findings.

A similar but more thorough study was conducted by Bruges (1988). She found that 22 per cent of the children who had been discharged from a language unit were still in some form of special education. The children's current teachers were asked to rate their academic achievement and social skills. For academic attainment,

21 per cent of the children were rated as 'average', 38 per cent as 'below average' and 40 per cent as being 'in the bottom 10 per cent'. In terms of social skills, 68 per cent of the children were rated as mixing well with their peers. Bruges argues that these findings suggest a better outcome than would be predicted from the findings of the National Child Development Study in which 50 per cent of children who had language problems at seven years showed residual language, learning, social and emotional problems at sixteen years (Sheridan and Peckham, 1978). However, the validity of such a comparison is highly questionable since it is unclear how Sheridan and Peckham's category of 'residual problems' maps on to the rating categories used in Bruges' study. Furthermore, as Bruges herself points out, her findings do not permit any conclusions to be drawn about which aspects of language unit provision were responsible for any beneficial effects, nor about which types of children were most likely to benefit.

On the basis of the currently available evidence, the verdict on the efficacy of language units has to be 'not proven'. Indeed, obtaining conclusive evidence on the efficacy of language units is a far from straightforward task. As the survey of Scottish language units showed, there are considerable variations amongst language units in both practice and policy, so it may not be meaningful to ask about the efficacy of language unit provision in general. There are also difficulties in identifying suitable groups of children with whom children in language units could be compared to evaluate the efficacy of language unit provision. One of the common reasons for selecting particular children for placements in a language unit is that their language difficulties are severe and have not responded to speech and language therapy prior to admission to the unit. Therefore, such children are by definition likely to differ from other children with specific language impairments who are in other forms of educational provision (such as mainstream schools). If group studies are to be carried out, it is essential to consider how the groups compare on a range of measures taken before the language unit placement begins, as well as assessing how much change occurs during and after the period of intervention. However, a more fruitful initial approach to addressing questions about the efficacy of language units might be to conduct a series of case studies in which the progress of individual children would be closely monitored before, during and after placement in particular language units and in which the nature of provision in these language units would be documented in detail. An interesting issue for such research to explore would be the quality of the interactions experienced by children with language disorders before and after the transition from a language unit to a mainstream school. There is a suggestion in the currently available evidence that children with language disorders may experience more success in achieving their communicative goals when they are conversing with another child who also has a language disorder rather than with a normally developing peer (Grove, Conti-Ramsden and Donlan, 1993). If this is indeed the case, then helping language unit children to develop their strategies for peer interaction might facilitate the transition to a mainstream school.

6.6 Overview and Implications

The approach to intervention which has been advocated here is one which is eclectic and individualized, but principled in that it is rooted in clearly specified goals. These goals, in turn, are derived from thorough, ongoing assessments of the strengths and weaknesses of the individual child. Compromise approaches to intervention are eclectic in that they aim to combine the advantages of behavioural and naturalistic techniques, by targeting particular linguistic structures within meaningful communicative contexts. When planning appropriate intervention for children with language impairments, there is a need for flexibility in considering the potential benefits of alternative models of service delivery and of collaboration, both with parents and with other professionals. Surveys of language units have been discussed in some detail here because they highlight several important issues, for example regarding collaboration and the nature of specific language impairment. It is clear from these surveys that even within this one type of setting, there is considerable variation in the nature of the provision and in the characteristics of individual children. Consequently, evaluating the effectiveness of a particular intervention setting, such as language units, is a far from straightforward task. Nevertheless, monitoring and evaluating the effectiveness of intervention techniques and settings is a crucial element of good professional practice. Both the importance and the complexity of evaluating professional practice are recognized by the College of Speech and Language Therapists in their publication *Communicating Quality* (1991), which provides professional standards and examples of good practice, while taking into account the diversity of service locations, client groups and types of disorders.

CHAPTER 7

In Conclusion

This book has reviewed some of the research evidence on children with language impairments and has tried to highlight the implications for professional practice. In particular, it has been argued that children with language impairments constitute a heterogeneous group, in terms of the severity of the disorder, the aspects of language ability which are impaired and the extent to which non-linguistic abilities are also affected. This implies that approaches to intervention need to be geared to the strengths and weaknesses of the individual child and therefore that they must be closely integrated with thorough, ongoing assessment procedures.

Having so far focused mainly on how professional practice can be informed by research findings, it is now time to turn to a consideration of two equally important aspects of the interface between practice and research.

The principles which underlie scientific research have much in common with those which underlie good practice by professionals in meeting the needs of children with language impairments. In conducting research, scientists formulate hypotheses which they then systematically test by collecting and analysing evidence. Very often, the empirical evidence leads scientists to revise their hypotheses and theories, and these in turn require to be tested through further data collection and analysis. In designing research studies, scientists will usually be guided by existing scientific theories and evidence, but they will also be prepared to challenge established views when these come into conflict with new evidence. Good scientific research typically involves a blend of many hours of painstaking, analytical work, along with occasional bursts of creative, intuitive thinking. Similarly, in order to provide appropriate intervention for children with language impairments the practitioner must seek to understand the nature of the individual child's difficulties. This involves formulating theories, hypotheses and questions on the basis of previous experience and knowledge of research findings, and then systematically testing these through the use of carefully selected assessment procedures and thoughtful analysis of the child's performance. The results of the initial assessments will help the practitioner to formulate further hypotheses about the intervention goals and techniques which are most likely to be appropriate. These hypotheses in their turn require to be tested by monitoring the effects of intervention and making modifications where necessary. Like the good scientist, the good practitioner will engage in a mixture of analytical and creative thinking and will be guided by, but not constrained by, 'established' knowledge.

As will be evident from the preceding chapters, many puzzles remain to be solved regarding children with language impairments. Practitioners have a crucial role to play in contributing to the further research which is required to tackle these puzzles. First, since they are closely involved in working with children who have language impairments they are very well placed to identify research questions with clear practical significance. Second, in view of the diversity of children's language impairments, detailed case studies may prove to be just as valuable as large scale group studies. Given the overlap between research and clinical skills, some extra documentation and analysis may sometimes be all that is required to convert routine case work into case studies. Third, academic researchers sometimes ask practitioners to participate in data collection for larger scale studies, such as a recent efficacy study of Metaphon (Reid *et al.* in press). Finally, practitioners sometimes conduct large-scale studies themselves, such as the longitudinal study of children at Dawn House (a special school for children with language impairments) which was carried out by a speech and language therapist and a headteacher/educational psychologist (Haynes and Naidoo, 1991). Of course, time and resource constraints often restrict the scale of projects which individual practitioners can feasibly conduct. Collaboration with researchers in academic institutions, who usually have more access to research facilities, can help to circumvent some of these constraints. Many practitioners are already making very positive contributions to research, but there is scope for many more to become involved.

A stronger interactive relationship between practice and research would be a powerful tool for helping children with language impairments to fulfil their potential.

References

Adams, C. (1990) Syntactic comprehension in children with expressive language impairment. *British Journal of Disorders of Communication 25*, 149–71.

Adams, C. and Bishop, D.V.M. (1989) Conversational characteristics of children with semantic–pragmatic disorder. 1: Exchange structure, turntaking, repairs and cohesion. *British Journal of Disorders of Communication 24*, 211–39.

Aitken, K.J., Papoudi, D., Robarts, J.Z. and Trevarthen, C. (1993) *Children with Autism.* Edinburgh: Edinburgh Centre for Research in Child Development, University of Edinburgh. Report to Scottish Office Education Department.

Anthony, A., Bogle, D., Ingram, T.T.S. and McIsaac, M.W. (1971) *The Edinburgh Articulation Test.* Edinburgh: Livingstone.

Aram, D.M., Ekelman, B.L. and Nation, J.E. (1984) Preschoolers with language disorders: ten years later. *Journal of Speech and Hearing Research 27*, 232–44.

Baron-Cohen, S. (1991) The theory of mind deficit in autism: How specific is it? *British Journal of Developmental Psychology 9*, 301–14.

Bates, E., Bretherton, I. and Snyder, L. (1988) *From First Words to Grammar: Individual Differences and Dissociable Mechanisms.* Cambridge: Cambridge University Press.

Beitchman, J.H., Nair, R., Clegg, M. and Patel, P.G. (1986) Prevalence of speech and language disorders in 5-year-old kindergarten children in the Ottawa-Carleton Region. *Journal of Speech and Hearing Disorders 51*, 98–110.

Bellugi, U., Marks, S., Bihrle, A. and Sabo, H. (1993) Dissociation between language and cognitive functions in Williams syndrome. In D. Bishop and K. Mogford (eds) *Language Development in Exceptional Circumstances*. Hove: Lawrence Erlbaum Associates.

Bellugi, U., van Hoek, K., Lillo-Martin, D. and O'Grady, L. (1993) The acquisition of syntax and space in young deaf signers. In D. Bishop and K. Mogford (eds) *Language Development in Exceptional Circumstances*. Hove: Lawrence Erlbaum Associates.

Bishop, D. (1983) *Test for Reception of Grammar*. Published by the author, Psychology Department, University of Manchester.

Bishop, D. (1989) Autism, Asperger's syndrome and semantic–pragmatic disorder: Where are the boundaries? *British Journal of Disorders of Communication 24*, 107–21.

Bishop, D. (1992) The underlying nature of specific language impairment. *Journal of Child Psychology and Psychiatry 33*, 3–66.

Bishop, D. (1993) Language development in children with abnormal structure or function of the speech apparatus. In D. Bishop and K. Mogford (eds) *Language Development in Exceptional Circumstances*. Hove: Lawrence Erlbaum Associates.

Bishop, D. (1994) Grammatical errors in specific language impairment: Competence or performance limitations? *Applied Psycholinguistics 15*, 507–50.

Bishop, D. and Adams, C. (1989) Conversational characteristics of children with semantic–pragmatic disorder. II: What features lead to a judgement of inappropriacy? *British Journal of Disorders of Communication 24*, 241–63.

Bishop, D. and Adams, C. (1990) A prospective study of the relationship between specific language impairment, phonological disorders and reading retardation. *Journal of Child Psychology and Psychiatry 31*, 1027–50.

Bishop, D. and Edmundson, A. (1987) Language-impaired 4-year-olds: distinguishing transient from persistent impairment. *Journal of Speech and Hearing Disorders 52*, 156–73.

Bishop, D. and Rosenbloom, L. (1987) Classification of childhood language disorders. In W. Yule and M. Rutter (eds) *Language Development and Disorders*. Oxford: MacKeith Press/Blackwell.

Bloom, L. (1974) Talking, understanding and thinking. In R. L. Schiefelbusch and L. L. Lloyd (eds) *Language Perspectives: Acquisition, Retardation and Intervention*. London: Macmillan.

Bochner, S., Price, P., Salmon, L., Yeend, G. and Orr, E. (1980) Language intervention: a classroom report. *British Journal of Disorders of Communication 15*, 87–102.

Bonvillian, J., Orlansky, M. and Novack, L. (1983) Development milestones: Sign language acquisition and motor development. *Child Development 54*, 1435–45.

Broen, P.A. and Westman, M.J. (1990) Project parent: a preschool speech program implemented through parents. *Journal of Speech and Hearing Disorders 55*, 495–502.

Bruges, A. (1988) The outcome of language unit placement: a survey in Avon 1987. *Educational Psychology in Practice 4*, 86–90.

Bruner, J.S. (1983) *Child's Talk: Learning to Use Language*. Oxford: Oxford University Press.

Camaioni, L., Castelli, M.C., Longobardi, E. and Volterra, V. (1991) A parent report instrument for early language assessment. *First Language 11*, 345–59.

Cantwell, D., Baker, L., Rutter, M. and Mawhood, L. (1989) Infantile autism and developmental receptive dysphasia: a comparative follow-up into middle childhood. *Journal of Autism and Developmental Disorders 19*, 19–32.

Cantwell, D.P. and Baker, L. (1987) *Developmental speech and language disorders*. London: Guilford Press.

Chomsky, N. (1986) *Knowledge of Language: It's Nature, Origin and Use*. New York: Praeger.

Clark, E.V. and Hecht, B.F. (1983) Comprehension, production and language acquisition. *Annual Review of Psychology 34*, 325–49.

Cole, K.N., Dale, P.S. and Mills, P.E. (1990) Defining language delay in young children by cognitive referencing; are we saying more than we know? *Applied Psycholinguistics 11*, 291–302.

College of Speech and Language Therapists (1991) *Communicating Quality: Professional Standards for Speech and Language Therapists*. London: College of Speech and Language Therapists.

Conant, S., Budoff, M., Hecht, B. and Morse, R. (1984) Language intervention: a pragmatic approach. *Journal of Autism and Developmental Disorders 14*, 301–17.

Conti-Ramsden, G., Donlan, C. and Grove, J. (1992) Characteristics of children with specific language impairment attending language units. *European Journal of Disorders of Communication 27*, 325–42.

Cromer, R.F. (1991) *Language and Thought in Normal and Handicapped Children.* Oxford: Blackwell.

Crystal, D. (1982) *Profiling Linguistic Disability.* London: Edward Arnold.

Crystal, D., Fletcher, P. and Garman, M. (1976) *The Grammatical Analysis of Language Disability: A Procedure for Assessment and Remediation.* London: Edward Arnold.

Curtiss, S. and Tallal, P. (1991) On the nature of the impairment in language-impaired children. In J.F. Miller (ed) *Research on Child Language Disorders: A Decade of Progress.* Austin, Texas: Pro-Ed.

Dale, P.S., Bates, E., Reznick, J.S. and Morisset, C. (1989) The validity of a parent report instrument of child language at twenty months. *Journal of Child Language 16*, 239–49.

Davis, J., Elfenbein, J., Schum, R. and Bentler, R. (1986) Effects of mild and moderate hearing impairments on language, educational and psychosocial behaviour of children. *Journal of Speech and Hearing Disorders 51*, 53–62.

Dewart, H. and Summers, S. (1988) *The Pragmatics Profile of Early Communication Skills.* Windsor: NFER-Nelson.

Dodd, B. (1976) A comparison of the phonological systems of mental age-matched normal, subnormal and Down's syndrome children. *British Journal of Disorders of Communication 11*, 27–42.

Dodd, B., Leahy, J. and Hambly, G. (1989) Phonological disorders in children: underlying cognitive deficits. *British Journal of Developmental Psychology 7*, 55–71.

Donaldson, M. (1978) *Children's Minds.* Glasgow: Collins/Fontana.

Donaldson, M.L. (1986) *Children's Explanations: A Psycholinguistic Study.* Cambridge: Cambridge University Press.

Donaldson, M.L. and Laing, K. (1993) Children's comprehension and production of locative expressions. In D. Messer and G. Turner (eds)

Critical Influences on Child Language Acquisition and Development.
London: Macmillan.

Donlan, C. (1987) Adequate provision? The ICAA survey of language
units. In J. Stone and M. Kersner (eds) *Language Units – A Review.*
London: National Hospital's College of Speech Sciences.

Drillien, C. and Drummond, M. (1983) *Development Screening and the
Child with Special Needs.* London: Heinemann Medical.

Dunn, L.M., Dunn, C., Whetton, C. and Pintillie, O. (1982) *The British
Picture Vocabulary Scale.* Windsor: NFER-Nelson.

Elliot, C.D., Murray, D.J. and Pearson, L.S. (1978) *British Ability Scales.*
Windsor: NFER-Nelson.

Enderby, P. and Davies, P. (1989) Communication disorders: planning
a service to meet the needs. *British Journal of Disorders of Communication
24*, 301–31.

Fay, W.H. (1993) Infantile autism. In D. Bishop and K. Mogford (eds)
Language Development in Exceptional Circumstances. Hove: Lawrence
Erlbaum Associates.

Fey, M.E. (1986) *Language Intervention with Young Children.* London:
Taylor and Francis.

Fowler, A. (1990) Language abilities in children with Down syndrome:
evidence for a specific syntactic delay. In D. Cicchetti and M.
Beeghly (eds) *Children with Down Syndrome.* Cambridge: Cambridge
University Press.

Fundudis, T., Kolvin, I. and Garside, R.F. (1979) *Speech Retarded and
Deaf Children: Their Psychological Development.* London: Academic Press.

Gardner, H. (1983) *Frames of Mind.* New York: Basic Books.

Gathercole, S.E. and Baddeley, A.D. (1990) Phonological memory
deficits in language disordered children: Is there a causal connection?
Journal of Memory and Language 29, 336–60.

Gathercole, S.E. and Baddeley, A.D. (1993) *Working Memory and
Language.* Hove, East Sussex: Lawrence Erlbaum Associates.

German, D.J. and Simon, E. (1991) Analysis of children's word-finding
skills in discourse. *Journal of Speech and Hearing Research 34*, 309–16.

Gibbard, D. (1994) Parental-based intervention with pre-school
language-delayed children. *European Journal of Disorders of
Communication 29*, 131–50.

Gopnik, M. and Crago, M. (1991) Familial aggregation of a developmental language disorder. *Cognition 39*, 1–50.

Grieve, R., Thomson, G., Donaldson, M.L., Dean, E., Millar, S., Reid, J. and Tait, L. (forthcoming) *The Role of Speech and Language Therapists in the Education of Pupils with Special Educational Needs.* Edinburgh: University of Edinburgh. Report to Scottish Office Education Department.

Grove, J., Conti-Ramsden, G. and Donlan, C. (1993) Conversational interaction and decision-making in children with specific language impairment. *European Journal of Disorders of Communication 28*, 141–52.

Grunwell, P. (1975) The phonological analysis of articulation disorders. *British Journal of Disorders of Communication 10*, 31–42.

Grunwell, P. (1981) *The Nature of Phonological Disability in Children.* London: Academic Press.

Harris, J. (1988) *Language Development in Schools for Children with Severe Learning Difficulties.* London: Croom Helm.

Harris, J. (1990) *Early Language Development: Implications for Clinical and Educational Practice.* London: Routledge.

Haynes, C. and Naidoo, S. (1991) *Children with Specific Speech and Language Impairment.* Oxford: MacKeith Press/Blackwell.

Hegde, M., Noll, M. and Pecora, R. (1979) A study of some factors affecting generalization of language training. *Journal of Speech and Hearing Disorders 44*, 301–20.

Hobson, R.P. (1991) Against the theory of 'Theory of Mind'. *British Journal of Developmental Psychology 9*, 33–51.

Howell, J. and Dean, E. (1994) *Treating Phonological Disorders in Children: Metaphon – Theory to Practice.* London: Whurr.

Howlin, P. (1987) Behavioural approaches to language. In W. Yule and M. Rutter (eds) *Language Development and Disorders.* Oxford: MacKeith Press/Blackwell.

Howlin, P. (1989) Changing approaches to communication training with autistic children. *British Journal of Disorders of Communication 24*, 151–68.

Howlin, P. and Kendall, L. (1991) Assessing children with language tests – which tests to use? *British Journal of Disorders of Communication 26*, 355–67.

Hyde Wright, S. (1993) Teaching word-finding strategies to severely language-impaired children. *European Journal of Disorders of Communication 28*, 165–75.

Ingram, D. (1976) *Phonological Disability in Children*. London: Edward Arnold.

Johnston, J.R. (1991) Questions about cognition in children with specific language impairment. In J.E. Miller (ed) *Research on Child Language Disorders*. Austin, Texas: Pro-Ed.

Jordan, R. (1993) The nature of the linguistic and communicative difficulties of children with autism. In D. Messer and G. Turner (eds) *Critical Influences on Child Language Acquisition and Development*. London: Macmillan.

Kiernan, C. (1987) Non-vocal communication systems: a critical survey. In W. Yule and M. Rutter (eds) *Language Development and Disorders*. Oxford: MacKeith Press/Blackwell.

Klein, S. and Rapin, I. (1993) Intermittent conductive hearing loss and language development. In D. Bishop and K. Mogford (eds) *Language Development in Exceptional Circumstances*. Hove: Lawrence Erlbaum Associates.

Knowles, W. and Masidlover, M. (1982) *Derbyshire Language Scheme*. Ripley, Derbyshire: Educational Psychology Service.

Lahey, M. (1988) *Language Disorders and Language Development*. London: Collier Macmillan.

Lahey, M. (1990) Who shall be called language disordered? Some reflections and one perspective. *Journal of Speech and Hearing Disorders 55*, 612–20.

Leahy, J. and Dodd, B. (1987) The development of disordered phonology: a case study. *Language and Cognitive Processes 2*, 115–32.

Lees, J. and Urwin, S. (1991) *Children with Language Disorders*. London: Whurr.

Leonard, L.B. (1981) Facilitating linguistic skills in children with specific language impairment. *Applied Psycholinguistics 2*, 89–118.

Leonard, L.B. (1987) Is specific language impairment a useful construct? In S. Rosenberg (ed) *Advances in Applied Psycholinguistics, volume 1: Disorders of First-Language Development*. Cambridge: Cambridge University Press.

Leonard, L.B. and Dromi, E. (1994) The use of Hebrew verb morphology by children with specific language impairment and children developing language normally. *First Language 14*, 283–304.

Leonard, L.B., McGregor, K.K. and Allen, G.D. (1992) Grammatical morphology and speech perception in children with specific language impairment. *Journal of Speech and Hearing Research 35*, 1076–85.

Leonard, L.B., Sabbadini, L., Leonard, J. and Volterra, V. (1987) Specific language impairment in children: a crosslinguistic study. *Brain and Language 32*, 233–52.

Letts, C.A. and Reid, J. (1994) Using conversational data in the treatment of pragmatic disorder in children. *Child Language Teaching and Therapy 10*, 1–22.

Lindner, K. and Johnston, J.R. (1992) Grammatical morphology in language-impaired children acquiring English or German as their first language: A functional perspective. *Applied Psycholinguistics 13*, 115–29.

Lovaas, O.I., Koegel, R., Simmons, J. and Stevens, J. (1973) Some generalization and follow-up measures on autistic children in behavior therapy. *Journal of Applied Behaviour Analysis 6*, 131–66.

McLean, J.E. and Snyder-McLean, L.K. (1978) *A Transactional Approach to Early Language Training.* Columbus, Ohio: Merrill.

McTear, M.M. and Conti-Ramsden, G. (1992) *Pragmatic Disability in Children.* London: Whurr.

Messer, D.J. (1994) *The Development of Communication: From Social Interaction to Language.* Chichester: Wiley.

Miller, J.F. (1991) Research on language disorders in children: a progress report. In J.F. Miller (ed) *Research on Child Language Disorders: A Decade of Progress.* Austin, Texas: Pro-Ed.

Mogford, K. (1993) Oral language acquisition in the prelinguistically deaf. In D. Bishop and K. Mogford (eds) *Language Development in Exceptional Circumstances.* Hove: Lawrence Erlbaum Associates.

MorganBarry, R. (1994) The relationship between dysarthria and verbal dyspraxia in children. In M. Kersner and R. MorganBarry (eds) *Work in Progress: Volume 4.* London: The National Hospital's College of Speech Sciences.

Muller, D.J., Munro, S.M. and Code, C. (1981) *Language Assessment for Remediation*. London: Croom Helm.

Nye, C., Foster, S.H. and Seaman, D. (1987) Effectiveness of language intervention with the language/learning disabled. *Journal of Speech and Hearing Disorders 52*, 348–57.

Peckham, C.S. (1973) Speech defects in a national sample of children aged seven years. *British Journal of Disorders of Communication 8*, 2–8.

Quigley, S. and Paul, P. (1987) Deafness and language development. In S. Rosenberg (ed) *Advances in Applied Psycholinguistics, volume 1: Disorders of First Language Development*. Cambridge: Cambridge University Press.

Rapin, I. and Allen, D. (1983) Developmental language disorders: nosological considerations. In U. Kirk (ed) *Neuropsychology of Language, Reading and Spelling*. New York: Academic Press.

Rapin, I. and Allen, D.A. (1987) Developmental dysphasia and autism in preschool children: characteristics and subtypes. In *Proceedings of the First International Symposium on Specific Speech And Language Disorders in Children*, University of Reading: AFASIC.

Reid, J. and Donaldson, M.L. (1993) Specific language impairment: explanations and implications. In G. Reid (ed) *Specific Learning Difficulties (Dyslexia): Perspectives on Practice*. Edinburgh: Moray House Publications.

Reid, J., Donaldson, M.L., Howell, J., Dean, E.C. and Grieve, R. (in press) The effectiveness of therapy for child phonological disorder: the Metaphon approach. In M. Aldridge (ed) *Proceedings of the Child Language Seminar, 1994*. Clevedon: Multilingual Matters.

Renfrew, C.E. (1969) *The Bus Story: A Test of Continuous Speech*. Available from the author at North Place, Old Headington, Oxford.

Rescorla, L. (1989) The language development survey: a screening tool for delayed language in toddlers. *Journal of Speech and Hearing Disorders 54*, 587–99.

Rescorla, L., Hadicke-Wiley, M. and Escarce, E. (1993) Epidemiological investigation of expressive language delay at age two. *First Language 13*, 5–22.

Reynell, J. (1979) *Reynell Developmental Language Scales*. Windsor: NFER-Nelson.

Rice, M.L. and Oetting, J.B. (1993) Morphological deficits of children with SLI: evaluation of number marking and agreement. *Journal of Speech and Hearing Research 36*, 1249–57.

Rondal, J. (1987) Language development and mental retardation. In W. Yule and M. Rutter (eds) *Language Development and Disorders*. Oxford: MacKeith Press/Blackwell.

Rondal, J. (1993) Down's syndrome. In D. Bishop and K. Mogford (eds) *Language Development in Exceptional Circumstances*. Hove: Lawrence Erlbaum Associates.

Rutter, M. (1985) Infantile autism and other pervasive developmental disorders. In M. Rutter and L. Hersov (eds) *Child and Adolescent Psychiatry: Modern Approaches*. London: Blackwell Scientific.

Rutter, M. (1987) Assessment of language disorders. In W. Yule and M. Rutter (eds) *Language Development and Disorders*. Oxford: MacKeith Press/Blackwell.

Rutter, M. and Lord, C. (1987) Language disorders associated with psychiatric disturbance. In W. Yule and M. Rutter (eds) *Language Development and Disorders*. Oxford: MacKeith Press/Blackwell.

Rutter, M. and Mawhood, L. (1991) The long-term psychosocial sequelae of specific developmental disorders of speech and language. In M. Rutter and P. Casaer (eds) *Biological Risk Factors for Psychosocial Disorders*. Cambridge: Cambridge University Press.

Sheridan, M. (1973) Children of seven years with marked speech defects. *British Journal of Disorders of Communication 8*, 9–16.

Sheridan, M. and Peckham, C. (1978) Follow-up to 16 years of school children who had marked speech defects at 7 years. *Child: Care, Health and Development 4*, 145–57.

Shulman, B.B. (1985) *Test of Pragmatic Skills*. Arizona: Communication Skills Builders.

Silva, P.A. (1980) The prevalence, stability and significance of developmental language delay in preschool children. *Developmental Medicine and Child Neurology 22*, 768–77.

Silva, P.A. (1987) Epidemiology, longitudinal course and some associated factors: an update. In W. Yule and M. Rutter (eds) *Language Development and Disorders*. Oxford: MacKeith Press/Blackwell.

Silva, P.A., Justin, C., McGee, R. and Williams, S.M. (1984) Some developmental and behavioural characteristics of seven-year-old children with delayed speech development. *British Journal of Disorders of Communication 19*, 147–54.

Silva, P.A., McGee, R.O. and Williams, S.M. (1983) Developmental language delay from three to seven years and its significance for low intelligence and reading difficulties at age seven. *Developmental Medicine and Child Neurology 25*, 783–93.

Silva, P.A., Williams, S. and McGee, R.O. (1987) A longitudinal study of children with developmental language delay at age three: later intelligence, reading and behaviour problems. *Developmental Medicine and Child Neurology 29*, 630–40.

Stackhouse, J. (1992) Developmental verbal dyspraxia I: A review and critique. *European Journal of Disorders of Communication 27*, 19–34.

Stackhouse, J. and Snowling, M. (1992) Developmental verbal dyspraxia II: A developmental perspective on two case studies. *European Journal of Disorders of Communication 27*, 35–54.

Stackhouse, J. and Wells, B. (1993) Psycholinguistic assessment of developmental speech disorders. *European Journal of Disorders of Communication 28*, 331–48.

Stevenson, J. (1984) Predictive value of speech and language screening. *Developmental Medicine and Child Neurology 26*, 528–38.

Stevenson, J. and Richman, N. (1976) The prevalence of language delay in a population of three-year-old children and its association with general retardation. *Developmental Medicine and Child Neurology 18*, 431–41.

Tager-Flusberg, H. (1992) Autistic children's talk about psychological states: deficits in the early acquisition of a theory of mind. *Child Development 63*, 161–72.

Tallal, P., Stark, R. and Curtiss, S. (1976) Relation between speech perception and speech production impairment in children with developmental dysphasia. *Brain and Language 3*, 305–17.

Tallal, P., Stark, R. and Mellits, D. (1985) Identification of language-impaired children on the basis of rapid perception and production skills. *Brain and Language 25*, 314–22.

Tew, B. (1979) The Cocktail Party Syndrome in children with hydrocephalus and spina bifida. *British Journal of Disorders of Communication 14*, 89–101.

Urwin, S., Cook, J. and Kelly, K. (1988) Preschool language intervention: a follow-up study. *Child: Care, Health and Development 14*, 127–46.

Vetter, D.K. (1991) Needed: intervention research. In J. Miller (ed) *Research on Child Language Disorders: A Decade of Progress.* Austin, Texas: Pro-ed.

Ward, S. and Kellett, B. (1982) Language disorder resolved? *British Journal of Disorders of Communication 17*, 33–52.

Watson, J. (1990) Language facilitation in the classroom. *British Journal of Special Education 17*, 143–7.

Weschler, D. (1974) *Weschler Intelligence Scale for Children.* New York: Psychological Corporation.

Working Party of Scottish Principal Educational Psychologists (1988) *Children with Communication Difficulties.* Available from Dr J. Watson, Moray House Institute of Education, Edinburgh.

Glossary

Aetiology Study of the cause of disease or disorder.

Alternative communication system A communication system which is used in place of spoken language, for example by deaf children or by children with severe dysarthria. Alternative communication systems include sign languages, sign systems, pictorial systems and written language (*augmentative communication system*).

Apraxia of speech *verbal dyspraxia.*

Articulation disorder Difficulties in producing speech sounds.

Articulatory dyspraxia *verbal dyspraxia.*

Augmentative communication system A communication system other than spoken language which is used to supplement or support spoken communication. The same systems (such as sign languages, sign systems, pictorial systems and written language) may be used either as augmentative communication systems (to supplement spoken communication) or as alternative communication systems (to replace spoken communication).

Autism A disorder characterized by delayed or deviant communicative development, impaired social development, ritualistic or repetitive behaviours, and onset before 30 months of age.

Behavioural approaches to language intervention These approaches are based on the principles of learning theory and hence on the assumption that language can be learned through such processes as imitation, reinforcement, shaping, modelling and prompting.

'Cocktail party syndrome' A disorder characterized by spontaneous speech which is semantically or pragmatically odd in relation to the conversational context and by poor performance on formal tests of language comprehension, despite the ability to produce speech which is syntactically correct and complex.

Communication disorder/impairment Difficulties in sharing or exchanging feelings, ideas, information etc. with other people. Communication problems may be either specific to linguistic communication or may affect both linguistic and non-linguistic communication.

Comprehension disorders/impairments *receptive disorders/impairments*.

Delayed language development A form of language impairment in which language development is slower than average without being qualitatively different from 'normal' language development. (Some authors contrast language delay with *language disorder/impairment*, by restricting the latter term to problems involving atypical rather than simply delayed development. Here, we use language disorder/impairment as neutral with respect to the delayed/deviant distinction, and we contrast delayed with *deviant* language development).

Developmental dysphasia *specific language disorder/impairment*.

Deviant language development A form of language impairment in which language development is qualitatively different from the norm (rather than simply slower than the norm) and in which the errors made are atypical even of younger children.

Dysarthria A disorder involving problems in the articulation of speech which are due to neurological problems (such as cerebral palsy) which prevent satisfactory control of the muscles involved in speech production.

Dysphasia *specific language disorder / impairment.*

Dysphonia A disorder of the voice, characterized by hoarseness.

Dyspraxia *verbal dyspraxia.*

Echolalia Repetition or echoing of what another person has said either immediately previously (***immediate echolalia***) or some time previously (***delayed echolalia***). Echolalia is particularly characteristic of (but not confined to) the speech of autistic children.

Elective mutism A refusal to speak in all but a few situations. The underlying causes of this disorder typically involve emotional disturbance or other psychiatric problems.

Expressive disorders / impairments These affect the child's own use of language, that is they apply to language production and to the child in the role of speaker.

Full-scale IQ *general intelligence.*

General intelligence A measure of intelligence which includes both verbal and non-verbal abilities. (Sometimes referred to as *full-scale IQ*).

General language disorder / impairment This occurs when both the receptive and the expressive functions of language are impaired, that is when there is difficulty both in understanding and in using language.

Generalization The process through which responses which are learned in one context are extended or transferred to other contexts.

Imitation A behavioural approach to language intervention in which the child is encouraged to imitate a word or sentence immediately after it has been produced by an adult.

Incidental learning Learning which occurs without explicit teaching and without the learner making a deliberate effort to acquire specific items of knowledge or specific skills.

Language A system of arbitrary, conventional symbols used to convey meanings. The symbols may take various forms, e.g. spoken. written, manual signs.

Language disorder/impairment Problems in using and/or understanding the system of conventional symbols which constitute a language. Here, the term language disorder/impairment is used to cover all such problems (whether phonological, syntactic, semantic or pragmatic), but some authors exclude articulation disorders from the category of language disorders/impairments.

Lexical Pertaining to individual words or items of vocabulary.

Lexicon A person's 'mental store' of vocabulary items.

Linguistic Pertaining to language.

Modelling A behavioural technique which is similar to imitation except that the child is not asked to reproduce the adult's utterance immediately. The child is asked to listen carefully while the adult produces (or *models*) the linguistic forms which are the target of intervention, and then the child is given a turn at speaking in a similar context.

Morpheme The smallest linguistic unit which has grammatical significance. For example, 'cats' consists of two morphemes: the noun stem 'cat' and the plural suffix '-s'.

Morphological Pertaining to morphemes. For example, morphological rules describe the way morphemes are combined to form words.

Naturalistic approaches to language intervention These are based on the assumption that children will learn language best in situations where it is being used to serve genuine communicative purposes and where it is closely integrated with real life activities. The role of the teacher or therapist usually involves facilitating incidental learning of linguistic forms in meaningful communicative contexts by providing appropriate linguistic input and encouraging the children to speak.

Non-linguistic communication This can be accomplished through for example touch, eye contact, gaze, facial expression and gesture. However, gestural communication is not always non-linguistic. If the gestures form a conventionalized, rule-governed system such as British Sign Language, then communication is linguistic.

Non-verbal intelligence (non-verbal IQ) Those aspects of a person's intelligence which are not dependent on linguistic skills or knowledge – for example, spatial abilities such as being able to arrange a set of blocks to form a particular pattern. (The terms non-verbal IQ and *performance IQ* are interchangeable.)

Performance IQ *non-verbal intelligence.*

Phoneme A speech sound (or more precisely a class of speech sounds) which contrasts with other speech sounds in a way which can convey a distinction in meaning. For example, in English [r] and [l] belong to different phonemes since the distinction between them can signal a meaning contrast (as in 'road' versus 'load'), whereas in Japanese these two speech sounds belong to the same phoneme since they are not used to signal differences in meaning.

Phonological Pertaining to phonology (that is to the speech sound system of a language).

Phonological disorders These consist of problems in perceiving and/or producing contrasts between phonemes. Sometimes such problems are specific to particular contexts (for example, the ends of words) and sometimes they involve difficulties with combining phonemes to form words.

Phonological processes These are systematic modifications to correct adult pronunciations which apply to classes of speech sounds and which usually involve simplification. An example of a phonological process is the deletion of final consonants. Phonological processes can occur both in normal and in disordered language development.

Phonology The system of speech sounds of a language. The phonological system is based on contrasts between phonemes and on rules for combining phonemes to form words.

Pragmatic Pertaining to pragmatics (that is to the communicative functions of language).

Pragmatic disorders These consist of impairments in children's ability to use language to fulfil various communicative purposes and/or in the ability to recognize the communicative intent underlying other people's use of language. Also, children with pragmatic disorders may have difficulties in making appropriate use of contextual cues and background knowledge to support their comprehension and production of language.

Pragmatics The ways language is used to fulfil communicative and social functions, such as persuading, gaining information, promising, threatening, requesting and commanding. Pragmatic aspects of language also include the influence of context on the meanings of words and sentences.

Production disorders/impairments *expressive disorders/impairments.*

Prompting A behavioural technique in which questions or commands are used to encourage the child to imitate or produce particular linguistic forms. Usually, the frequency of prompts is reduced as intervention proceeds.

Prosodic Pertaining to the pitch, intonation, loudness, tempo and rhythm of speech.

Receptive disorders/impairments These affect the child's understanding of the language produced by other people; that is, they apply to language comprehension and to the child in the role of hearer.

Reinforcement A behavioural technique in which a correct response by the child is followed by something which the child is likely to find pleasurable (a *reinforcer,* such as praise or a tangible reward) in order to increase the likelihood of the child producing the same response on subsequent occasions.

Semantic Pertaining to semantics (that is to meaning).

Semantic disorders These consist of difficulties in expressing and/or understanding meaning through language. For example, the child may have a limited number of words in her/his vocabulary, may have an incorrect understanding of the meaning of particular words, or may have difficulty retrieving appropriate words from her/his mental lexicon.

Semantics The system of meaning relations in a language. Semantic relations can hold between a word (or lexical item) and an object/event/attribute in the 'real' world. For example, the word 'chair' denotes a particular class of objects. Semantic relations (of a different type) can also hold between the words which make up a speaker's lexicon (or vocabulary). For example, words may contrast in meaning ('big/small') or may overlap in meaning ('dog/animal'). Of course, sentences as well as individual words have semantic properties. Hence the distinction between semantics and syntax is not always clearcut.

Shaping A behavioural technique in which the criteria for determining whether a response is reinforced as 'correct' are gradually made more stringent. Thus, initially any approximation to the correct response may be reinforced but later reinforcements will only be given for successively closer approximations to the correct response.

Sign language A system in which manual signs are the conventional symbols used to convey meanings. Sign languages have syntactic rules which sometimes differ from those of spoken English. Examples of sign languages include British Sign Language and American Sign Language.

Specific language disorder/impairment A language impairment in which the child's language problems are more severe than would be expected on the basis of his/her level of intelligence, and for which the aetiology is usually unclear. (Sometimes also referred to as: *developmental dysphasia, dysphasia* or *specific developmental language disorder*).

Speech disorder This term is used here to refer to difficulties in producing speech sounds. However, some authors use speech disorder in a more general way to refer to problems with any aspect of spoken language.

Syntactic Pertaining to syntax (that is to the grammatical properties of a language).

Syntactic disorders These affect the child's ability to produce grammatical sentences and/or to respond appropriately to the grammatical properties of other people's speech.

Syntax The system of grammatical (or syntactic) rules which describe the way words are combined to form sentences. Some authors also use *syntactic rules* to refer to the rules for combining grammatical elements smaller than a word (morphemes), for example in adding plural endings to nouns or past tense endings to verbs. Other authors refer to these as *morphological rules* and restrict the term *syntactic rules* to combinations of whole words. Here, we adopt the more general definition of 'syntactic'.

Verbal dyspraxia A disorder characterized by difficulty in programming the sequences of motor acts required to produce continuous speech, despite an ability to articulate individual speech sounds. (Sometimes referred to as *apraxia of speech, articulatory dyspraxia* or *dyspraxia*).

Verbal intelligence (verbal IQ) Those aspects of a person's intelligence which depend on linguistic skills or knowledge.

Subject Index

Author Index